BEST

of the

BLUE RIDGE PARKWAY

Text and Photography by
Nye Simmons

of the ***Friends***
BLUE RIDGE
PARKWAY
www.BlueRidgeFriends.org

Mountain Trail Press
www.mountaintrailpress.com

BEST *of the* BLUE RIDGE PARKWAY

Book design: Nye Simmons
Editor: Abbey Jones

Published by:
Mountain Trail Press
1818 Presswood Road
Johnson City, TN 37604

ISBN-13: 978-0-9777933-9-6
ISBN-10: 0-9777933-9-7
Printed in China.
First Printing, Spring 2008

Published in cooperation with

FRIENDS of the **Blue Ridge Parkway, Inc**.

Front cover: Blue Ridge Parkway from FR 816, near Graveyard Fields, MP 420.2.
Title Page: Sunbeams at Cowee Mountains Overlook, MP 430.7.
Right: Mountain laurel along the Fallingwater Cascades Trail, MP 83.1.

DISCLAIMER AND DENIAL OF LIABILITY
There are hazards both obvious and obscure any time you set foot on the Parkway, or leave your home for that matter. Weather and road hazards, hiking injuries and plain old-fashioned bad luck can befall at any time. The information in this book is a guide only and not a substitute for exercising good judgement in your travels. Hiking and driving safety are your responsibility. Neither the author nor the publisher assume any liability, expressed or implied for property damages or injuries that occur while visiting any location listed in this book or elsewhere.

The maps in this book were modified from the official Park Service map by the author and are believed to be accurate. Some of the modifications may not be to scale. These maps are for general overview and orientation purposes and are not a substitute for more detailed and complete maps for navigation. The National Park Service bears no responsibility for the maps in this book.

In Memory

Writing a memorial in a book is a bittersweet time as the thoughts and memories of loved ones now departed come to the fore. Those most recently gone seem freshest in thought, though none are loved any less. My parents, Charles and Lorraine, gave me boundless love and passed on a passion for the natural world and the written word. This book bears their fingerprints on every page. There are not thanks enough to give.

My niece, Jennifer Mosgrove, left this world far too young. May your soul find eternal peace and happiness.

My lifelong friend, Olivia Derousselle Mamou, now rests with her Lord, leaving behind many friends and relatives who miss her dearly. To her this book is dedicated. Cher, tu es en mon cœur.

ACKNOWLEDGEMENTS

Writing and producing a book is an all-consuming task in the best of situations, much less one covering such a vast area as the Blue Ridge Parkway. I could not have done it alone. Many folks deserve thanks and appreciation for their contributions to this project, more than space allows, and I apologize to those of you not mentioned here.

Cara Ellen Modisett, editor of *Blue Ridge Country* magazine, introduced me to Susan Mills, executive director of **FRIENDS** of the Blue Ridge Parkway. **FRIENDS** was the missing link that made this book complete, and opened a way to give back to the Parkway. Thank you both for all that you have done, and are continuing to do every day.

Debbie Pitts, executive director, and Eddie Goode, historian, at Virginia's Explore Park, provided a wealth of information about the Explore Park and area history. Speaking for myself, and for many: We wait with eager anticipation for the resumption of operations and wish all of you the very best.

Jesse Pope, naturalist at Grandfather Mountain, generously shared his knowledge of high country ecology as well as "what's happening now." Thanks, Jesse. Your help was priceless. Thanks to Crae Morton for insights into the Grandfather story and to all the Grandfather staff for the great work that you do.

Several staff members with the National Park Service gave critically important insights and corrected factual inaccuracies in the manuscript. Thank you for your gracious help with this book. There are many National Park Service staff members who work daily to make the Parkway a better place for all of us. Thanks to each of you at the Park Service for all that you do. Without you, the Parkway would cease to be.

Special thanks to the cartographic and design staff at the National Park Service Harpers Ferry Center who have made their work available to the public. That is a great service to a project such as this.

Thanks to Jerry Greer and Ian Plant, my friends and publishers at Mountain Trail Press, for supporting me and having faith in this book. Those many sunrises and sunsets have finally found their way to the printed page.

Thanks to Jennifer Bernabe and Cara Ellen Modisett (again) for design and content critique, and to Brian Wiehn for the camera icon for the photo notes.

Finally, thanks to my wife Deborah. You put up with my many road trips to the mountains, and the long hours spent in the office producing this book. It's almost done.

Many critters make their home on and near the Parkway. They are most active in the early and late hours of the day, just at a time when visibility is not its best. Each year many wild Parkway residents die from vehicular collisions.

Deer are the most commonly seen and frequently do the unexpected: After crossing the road they will reverse course when you think they are in the clear and jump right in front of your vehicle. There is often another deer that you don't see in the adjacent woods that wants to catch up to its buddies. Bambi that you can't see, will often run right in front of you. I guess it's their way of playing "chicken." Slow down immediately if you see deer near the roadside.

Best of the Blue Ridge Parkway

Best of the Blue Ridge Parkway

INTRODUCTION

The Blue Ridge Parkway is a magnificent ribbon of asphalt, 469 miles in length, traversing the southern Appalachians between Shenandoah and Great Smoky Mountains National Park. The Parkway is much more than a road; it is a concept, a living museum, a monument to the scenery and culture of our southern mountains. It connects the above two parks, offering an easily accessible scenic drive along the spine of the Blue Ridge Mountains and the valleys between and provides a different sort of experience from the traditional "park." It receives more visitation than any other unit in the National Park system. It is superb!

Conceived and executed many years ago at a time when the automobile was becoming affordable to ordinary people, it was hoped to be a means of enhancing tourism in the states it traversed. Construction continued long after the Great Depression ended and provided an honest day's work to many who were otherwise unemployed. It was to become a means to share the scenic wonders and unique cultural aspects of the southern Appalachians from the comfort of one's vehicle, accessible to all. Built over a period of more than 50 years, starting in 1935, the final link in the chain was closed on the flanks of Grandfather Mountain following the completion of the Linn Cove Viaduct in 1987. Now, 20 years later, the country has changed, the landscape has continually changed, and the entire length is taken for granted, the many challenges of its construction long forgotten. The history of many successes and failures has faded into obscurity, but the Parkway endures today, splendidly waiting for you.

We see a mature Parkway today that seems to be in its proper place, part of the land-scape, like it's supposed to be there. This is by design, not chance. Yet if it did not ex-ist, it probably would not exist. Imagine getting the necessary environmental waivers to construct such a thoroughfare through the mountains today. Impossible! Imagine the cost of construction and land acquisition in current dollars. Not likely! Paradigms and priorities change, yet today we can enjoy this magnificent roadway through the southern Appalachians that we probably would not now build.

The Blue Ridge Parkway will take you through dramatic elevation changes, from the low point in the valley of the James River at 649 feet to the Peaks of Otter at almost 4,000 feet in a few short miles. In North Carolina, a similar climb leads from the French Broad at Asheville, to the high country of the Mount Pisgah area and on to the Parkway high point at Richland Balsam, over 6,000 feet tall. Contrast indeed! On a spring day there may be snow on the peaks while the sun is shining brightly on dogwoods below. Elevation is everything here; there can be a different season a few miles away.

A love of these mountains brings many supporters together who otherwise have divergent economic, historic and recreational interests. The asphalt coursing through these high places does not provoke (most) lovers of wild places to complain too loudly about being able to drive to high trailheads or pedal the Parkway's steeps and valleys. Indeed, the Blue Ridge Parkway provides access to some of the finest wild

Cycling is increasingly popular on the Parkway. The safety of these riders should be of concern to all of us. The Parkway's many delightful curves can conceal riders from you until you are dangerously close to them. Be alert at all times for our two-wheeled friends.

places in the southern Appalachians, and provides it to all, not just the elite outdoor athlete. Anyone can enjoy a high mountain sunset with no more effort than turning a key in the ignition. Easy accessibility allows the Parkway to provide enjoyment for everyone.

The Blue Ridge Parkway is at once a national and a local treasure. Many residents near the Parkway think of it as "their" Parkway, it being in their backyard as it were. I apologize to those of you who know sections of the Parkway better than I ever will. I hope I have not left out your favorite spot, and that I have done justice to the rest.

The Parkway runs generally northeast to southwest. In the United States, our east-west highways are even-numbered, and north-south ones are odd-numbered. In this guidebook, directions given for odd-numbered roads will be north-south, and for even-numbered will be east-west. This may seem confusing at times – at some bends in the Parkway, logic and your compass may tell you something different.

SHARE THE ROAD

Cycling is a popular activity on the Blue Ridge Parkway, particularly near cities such as Asheville, Boone, Blowing Rock and Roanoke. A "ride," for the more athletic riders, may be a 50- or 60-mile round trip — finding bikes on the Mount Mitchell spur and in the Mount Pisgah area is quite common.

You can come upon them abruptly going around a curve, particularly when they are chugging slowly up a steep hill. If there is oncoming traffic, the situation can quickly become dangerous, even if your speed is not excessive. Be alert, and anticipate the potential for unexpected, slower-moving travelers, particularly when visibility is limited.

For many reasons, motorcycles need this same consideration; their lowered visibility puts them at increased risk. Motorcyclists need to be particularly careful on the Parkway's spiral curves. Accidents are becoming all too frequent.

Ridges stacked upon ridges receding into the infinite distance are a classic Parkway scene. This book will help you develop a strategy for seeing such sights while still having dinner and a place to stay.

Side trips "Off-Parkway"

These mountains failed to recognize geo-political or administrative boundaries before the first European settlers arrived, so I have taken the brash liberty of failing in similar fashion. The Blue Ridge Parkway today is managed like a national park, by the National Park Service, though the words "National Park" are absent from the name. Close by, sometimes adjacent to Parkway boundaries, lie many exceptional natural areas. Several of these have been considered "part of the Parkway" because they were previously featured in published photo essays and books.

Many of these scenic places seem "spiritually" a part of the Parkway experience, even though they are not technically within the narrow Parkway right of way. Most are under separate management by the U.S. Forest Service, with a few notable, privately held, attractions of interest. I have included carefully selected side trips that I think will enhance your Parkway experience.

Traveling the Parkway

The Parkway architects designed the thoroughfare to be very user friendly, with scenic overlooks, rest stops, picnic areas and services along the way at frequent intervals. Each chapter gives details about those locations.

Whether traveling by automobile or motorcycle, the basics are the same. The Parkway speed limit is 45 mph unless otherwise posted. This statutory limit is often trumped by that imposed by weather or other safety concerns. Safety often dictates a slower speed — safety for you as well as other Parkway visitors and residents. Many critters call the Parkway home; a collision with a deer can total your vehicle and makes a bad day for the deer.

Don't plan your day with an average speed of 45 mph in mind — an average of 30 or 35 mph is more like it. Understand that touring the Parkway is much like fine dining — don't rush through it.

Bad weather can produce exceptional scenes such as the cloud-enshrouded Looking Glass Rock, but brings additional hazards. Use caution and good judgement if attempting a high country drive in bad weather. Speeds often are reduced to 10 mph due to poor visibility; dense fog sometimes conceals the center stripe. High winds can topple a travel trailer or RV.

Weather

You will frequently see signs warning you to avoid the Parkway during snow, ice and fog. Snow and ice (usually) pose no special problem as the road closes as soon as safety becomes an issue. Standard road treatments are not allowed on Parkway lands for environmental reasons, and most visitors are not experienced drivers on treacherous icy mountain roads (if they were, they wouldn't need a sign—they would stay off). Fog is quite another matter; the driver is left to choose. "Fog" at higher elevations is really "cloud," as in being in a cloud, often with rain. It's not uncommon to be driving 10 mph, and navigating by the center stripe. You will notice the absence of the usual white stripes on the right hand side of the road; this design feature enhances the feel of being on a country lane. Exit the Parkway as soon as a crossroad allows, unless you have some pressing need to be driving 10 miles per hour with limited visibility.

Driving Etiquette

There are relatively few straightaways that will allow for safe passing of slow moving vehicles. Be aware of your speed and considerate of others; pull over at one the many overlooks or other pull-outs to allow others to pass. Parking on the shoulder is legal as long as it doesn't damage the turf. Avoid soft shoulders, you will cut up the turf trying to get back on the road. Wet grass is a trap for the unwary; you can easily get stuck or worse, leave an ugly scar that may take years to heal. If you do find yourself stuck and you have 4WD, use it to minimize the damage.

Leave no Trace

With over 20 million visitors annually, we all have to be careful with our trash. Many folks aren't aware of other impacts. Bears and other animals live here too, though you may not see them in mid-

Soco Gap MP 455 at 4340 feet elevation often catches the full force of winter storms. Access via U.S. 19 from Cherokee or Maggie Valley for winter fun. Nearby Cataloochee ski resort in Maggie offers lift served downhill skiing.

Winter Access

The high country is often the land of snow and ice, even when lower elevations are at more moderate temperatures. Access is limited for safety and environmental reasons. Peaks of Otter remains open year round, and Linville Falls is accessible from NC 183, when the Blue Ridge Parkway itself is closed. Those wanting a snow and ice experience at other locations can use crossroads for access to hike or even cross country ski along the Parkway itself. A few inches of snow creates a great ski trail over the pavement, and is still easy walking if you (like most of us) don't own skis. There is always ample parking space. Mountain driving can be quite treacherous during or after a winter storm. Travel at your own risk, taking all precautions.

day. Improper disposal of picnic supplies or the remains of that sandwich you had for lunch can lead to widespread trash after Mr. Yogi gets hold of it.

Human food is higher in fat content; animals like it and want more. They can become pests that have to be relocated or destroyed, and they are more likely to get hit by cars. They lose their natural fear of people and can become aggressive and more susceptible to poaching. If there is no nearby animal-proof receptacle, hold on to your trash until one is available.

Walking around many overlooks, you can find used tissues and often the occasional diaper in the bushes. If you must "go," use a plastic baggie to pack out your used tissues to the nearest appropriate receptacle.

ABOUT THIS BOOK

Parkway designers envisioned centers of interest and activity — "Jewels on a string of beads" was Parkway architect, Stanley Abbott's, term. Taken along with other highlights in the area, these "jewels" form the structure for this book and for planning a tour. I will take you on a written Parkway tour, with photos that give you a visual preview of what waits for you. You will find the necessary information to plan a casual or in-depth visit, with some (rough) estimates of how long a site visit might take to help you budget your time.

At the beginning of each chapter is a sectional map, modified for this book, and a table listing points of interest as well as local services — where to find gas, lodging, meals and medical services, followed by an overview and then location details. In the text, each featured location has pictographs indicating the available services and, in parentheses, the elevation. Much of what interests you, such as spring wildflowers and fall color, will be elevation-dependent on the Parkway.

I organized this book starting at the north entrance; while in sequence, each chapter can be an independent guide. Most visitors don't have time to see the entire Parkway on one visit and enter at some midway point.

Chapters one through eleven target each major scenic area as well as Parkway related attractions in, or near, the cities of Roanoke and Asheville. I included classic Parkway icons, less-well-known points of interest and several other worthwhile detours "off- Parkway."

A little walking is good for the soul; get out of the vehicle, breathe some fresh mountain air and stretch your legs. You will see wonderful sights that you would otherwise miss. I describe short hikes to scenic destinations that are not "death marches." If you don't hike at all, this book will entice you to put on some sturdy shoes to give it a try — it also tells you what's next around the bend if you wish to keep driving. A pictograph indicates wheelchair accessibility for those whose physical health restricts mobility; assistance may be needed at less developed sites.

A PERSONAL JOURNEY

My first drive along the Blue Ridge Parkway many years ago was a big disappointment. In a two -day trip leaving Shenandoah, I reached the edge of Great Smoky Mountains National Park wondering what all the fuss was about. Trying to cover that much ground in two days left no time to ponder, no time to take a side hike, even if I had a good idea which one to take; I passed many gorgeous locations, unimpressed because of bad light. I had missed much more than the point, I had missed most of what the Parkway has to offer. Indeed, there were detailed guides available then, but the information was *TOO* detailed. Milepost by milepost, the forest lay quietly amongst the trees as I drove by, hidden from my hurried view. Several years and countless miles later, after many secrets had been revealed, this book came to be. It distills the essence and the best features of this Blue Ridge Mountain thoroughfare to help you get the most enjoyment out of your visit. This is the guidebook that I wished for, when I made my first trip. RIGHT: The author contemplates evening light at Spy Rock, on the Appalachian Trail near Crabtree Falls.

1

the
First 30 Miles

Humpback Rocks

Farm Museum
Humpback Rocks
Appalachian Trail

Crabtree Falls

Priest Wilderness
Spy Rock
Appalachian Trail
St. Mary's Wilderness
and Falls

MP 0.0 - 30

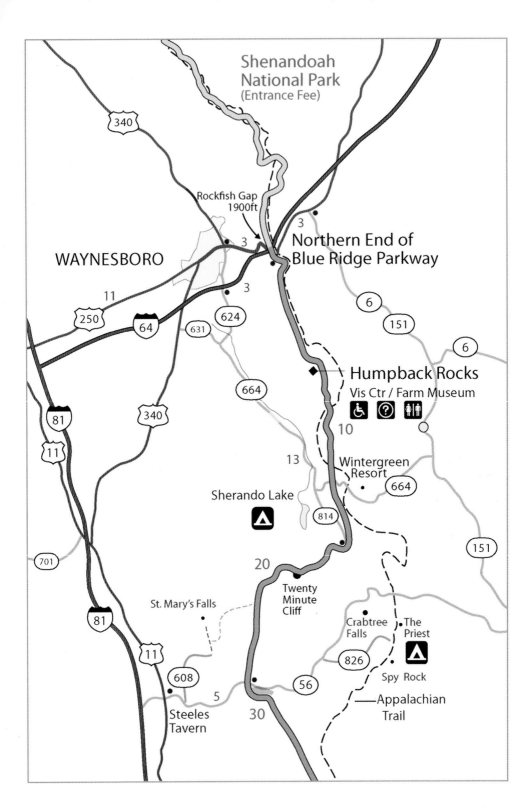

Simple pleasures like music, reading and storytelling helped pass idle time in the days before electronic media took over our lives.

MP	POINT OF INTEREST	FEATURES
5.9	Humpback Rocks Farm Museum	Historical structures, interpretive programs, visitor center
6.0	Humpback Rocks Trailhead	One mile hike to Humpback Rocks
8.3	Humpback Rocks Picnic Area	Picnic area
19	Twenty Minute Cliff Overlook	Scenic views, photography
exit 27	Crabtree Falls & Priest Wilderness, VA 56 – about 7 miles (E)	Hiking, photography (lowest cascade ♿ accessible with assist)
exit 27	St. Mary's Falls – VA 56 to Steeles Tavern, 5 miles west	Hiking, photography

MP	LODGING AND DINING	MP	CAMPING
0.0	Waynesboro via I-64 or U.S. 250 access leaving Rockfish Gap	exits 13.7 & 16	Sherando Lake – VA 664 and 814, about 4-5 miles west of BRP
13.7	Wintergreen Resort – 1 mile east	exit 27	Montebello (commercial)
27	Steeles Tavern VA 56 – 5 miles west	exit 27	Crabtree Meadows (primitive)

MP	GASOLINE	MP	HOSPITAL
0.0	Waynesboro – 2-3 miles Rockfish Gap – near entry	exit 0.0	Waynesboro – **Augusta Medical Center** 540-332-4000
exit 13.7	Wintergreen Resort – 1 mile (E)		
exit 27	Montebello VA 56 – 2 miles (E)		
exit 27	Steeles Tavern VA 56 – 5 miles west		

OVERVIEW

The Parkway starts off with a bang at a re-created mountain farm offering seasonal interpretive programs and extensive scenic and hiking options in just the first 30 miles. Off-Parkway hiking options include Priest and St. Mary's Wilderness areas and Spy Rock. Touring the Farm Museum, hiking up to Humpback Rocks and visiting Crabtree Falls can take most, if not all, of a day. You can squeeze it all in and still get to the Otter area for the night, but it requires an early start and careful planning. The casual visitor can blast through in a short morning; an in-depth visit could take a hiking enthusiast 2 or 3 days. Lodging options include hotels in Waynesboro, B&Bs near Steeles Tavern, camping at Sherando Lake, at Montebello on VA 56, and primitive, no-fee camping near Crabtree Meadows on VA 826. Wintergreen Resort, 1 mile south of the Parkway(exit at MP 13.7 east onto VA 664) features high- end lodging and a range of dining options. There is no food service on this section, so plan accordingly.

A good supply of stove wood was an everyday necessity of farm life.

 5.9 **Humpback Farm Museum (2,360)**
⊙ 🚻 🚶 ♿

You will soon reach Humpback Farm Museum after entering the Parkway at Rockfish Gap. The visitor center is a great opportunity to further research your visit, and provides a chance to stretch your legs and maybe even learn something while you tour the farm. The Mountain Farm exhibit is a re-created farmstead comprised of relocated authentic structures that creates a realistic representation of a 19th-century mountain farmstead. Many such farms remained little changed until after World War II. Interpretive staff add a living touch to this exhibit during the summer and fall months when the program specialists are available. Imagine yourself transported back to a time when self-sufficiency was a way of life, not a "new-age" notion. We've come a long way since those difficult times our forefathers lived in, and we have lost something in the process. Here the memory is kept alive. The tour can be as brief or detailed as your interest and time budget allow. Hikers may wish to continue through to the Humpback Rocks trailhead at nearby Humpback Gap (an additional 0.1 mile) or you can return to your vehicle, make any of those last-minute stops at the visitor center, and continue on your way.

Allow 30 minutes to 2-3 hours.

A setting moon graces the namesake Humpback Rocks as seen from the Mountain Farm.

6.0 Humpback Rocks (2,360) 🚶

The trailhead and parking area at Humpback Gap serves the Humpback Rocks and provides access to the Appalachian Trail. Fit hikers can make the short but steep climb to the rocks for expansive views. It is roughly a mile one-way with about a 700-foot vertical elevation gain to the summit. At about 0.5 miles you will reach an intersection with a square post having blue blazes; the old trail turns left, rising steeply uphill. The old trail is badly eroded and has been re-routed straight ahead. Continue straight to an intersection with the summit trail and the AT. To reach the summit, turn left, back to the north. To the right, the AT treads south to the summit of Humpback Mountain in another mile, and the picnic area in two additional miles.

The rocks are worn slick in many places from countless visitors, but the real tragedy is the senseless defacement with spray paint. This graffiti reflects poorly on us as a society and a nation, and severely detracts from the otherwise superb views.

Most visitors will hike to the "Rocks" and return the same way they went up. Sturdy hiking shoes (preferably hiking boots) are a good idea, though some have hiked it wearing sandals.

It's at least a one-hour round-trip hike if you are quite fit, more if you are not used to hiking on steep ground. Once there, thirty minutes to poke around the rocks and snap some photos is a minimum.

PHOTO NOTES

Photographers: *Allow at least 90 minutes to hike and scout for your image. Be prepared to photograph at least one hour before actual sunset to watch the play of light on the rocks and the land below before it all goes into shadow.*

exit 16 — Sherando Lake Recreation Area

Access via VA 814 (or VA 664, MP 13.7), and drive about 4.5 miles off Parkway. This forest service-managed area offers several hiking trails, fishing, rest rooms, and provides one of the few camping options in the area. Photographers note: The gate is locked at night—it re-opens at dawn. Anyone planning a sunrise experience on Humpback Rocks will need to stay somewhere else. Sherando can be a destination, or a hub for exploring this end of the Parkway and surrounding areas. Return to the Parkway to reach Twenty Minute Cliff and beyond.

19 — Twenty Minute Cliff (2,715)

This special overlook offers a bit of history as well as superb views. Story has it that folks in the White Rock Community used the cliff as a time piece. In June and July, during corn chopping time, dusk would fall in the valley below, 20 minutes after last light hit the rock face. The cliff today offers a nearly pristine view of the ridges and valleys to the west; the few signs of modern life are well hidden in the valley below. The heavily developed countryside along both flanks of the Blue Ridge Crest rarely permits such an elemental view. This, coupled with

Late April brings color and life to bare trees on the Parkway. LEFT: Early spring green graces the ridges as seen from Humpback Rocks. TOP: Sarvis adds a touch of color to the cliffs at Humpback Rocks. BOTTOM: An outbuilding typical of the period graced by spring dogwoods at the Mountain Farm, MP 5.9.

Fresh spring foliage glows neon in afternoon light along the ridges below Twenty Minute Cliff Overlook, MP 19.

attractive lines and a westward facing exposure, makes this an excellent location for evening photography.

Allow at least a few minutes unless photographing.

Photo Notes

Serious photographers consider this the best evening light location in the area. It's ideal more than an hour before sunset because the valley below goes into shadow late in the evening. For full light on the valley below, get there a bit earlier than you think you need

to. For those indulging in sunset here, meal options are limited to the 30-minute drive to Waynesboro, dining at Wintergreen or what you brought with you. You won't make Peaks of Otter Lodge while they are still serving dinner in the spring, and maybe not in the fall.

Such unspoiled views are under constant threat; once construction starts, it's hard to tear it all down and erase the damage. The challenge of preserving "view-sheds" is integral to the ongoing success of managing the Parkway for current and future generations.

OFF PARKWAY

exit 27 Crabtree Falls 🚶 🚻 ♿

Continue to MP 27, exit the Parkway east on VA 56 and drive about seven miles of steep winding road to reach Crabtree Falls. Don't confuse this waterfall with the North Carolina falls of the same name. Crabtree Creek comes off the high slopes of the Priest, in Priest Wilderness Area. It gives rise to one of the most spectacular cascades in the east in its breakneck dash to the valley below. Whether your passion is hiking, sightseeing, photography—or all three, Crabtree will satisfy.

It is one of the claimants to "highest waterfall in the east." If one counts total drop in series, as opposed to one clean single falls, at nearly 1,500 vertical feet, it may well be true. It is a Forest Service fee area; a modest fee buys the right of entry to this exquisite area and contributes to maintaining visitor facilities. A short wheelchair-accessible trail leads to the base of the lowest cascade and a viewing platform.

From there it is a steep, switch-backing, stair-stepping trail following the falls up cascade after cascade. Eventually, after three steep miles, you reach the upper trailhead on VA 826, where no-camping signs are posted. Crabtree Meadows is not signed as such, and one could easily mistake the upper trailhead for it. Camping is allowed at multiple primitive sites close by. From here you can access the AT into Priest Wilderness to the North and Spy Rock to the South, adding about three and five miles round-trip respectively, for a very long day of hiking. Vehicle permitting, you could drive to the upper trail head and have a central access point for all three hikes. Alternatively, turn around at whatever point you like, and "coast" back to your car. The cascades can bemuse waterfall lovers and photographers for hours.

Several commercial campgrounds serve the area, both before and after reaching the falls on VA 56. The hamlet of Montebello offers a commercial campground and is a little less than three miles from the Parkway exit.

Allow 10-15 minutes driving time from the Parkway. Give yourself five minutes to walk to the base of the falls. Plan 3-4 hours to hike to the top and return, longer if photographing, and 6-8 hours if continuing on to hike on the AT.

WARNING

The falls are coated with an algae, nearly invisible, slicker than motor oil. Many have fallen to their deaths here climbing on the rocks around the falls. Do not venture onto the rocks for a "better look." Stay behind the guard rails.

---

exit 27 St. Mary's Falls and Wilderness 🚶 🏕

St. Mary's Falls are most easily accessed from VA 56, though a trailhead on the Parkway itself is an option. St. Mary's Falls are the best-known feature, but that's only one of several reasons to visit this, the largest federally designated wilderness area in the state of Virginia. Miles of hiking trails give you extended trip planning options. Maps are essential as a detailed description exceeds the scope of this book.

LEFT: Crabtree Falls reveals its magic in the peak of autumn color.

RIGHT: St. Mary's Falls, still gorgeous in a drought year.

BELOW: Rock formations glow in the fading light of an October sunset at the Priest summit in Priest Wilderness. It's about a 1.5-mile hike from the Crabtree Meadows parking area.

Short ventures from the Parkway bring many splendid hiking opportunities with magnificent scenery.

SIDE TRIPS FOR THE ADVENTUROUS

The drive to Crabtree Meadows is not for everyone, but it offers several outstanding hiking options. You can get there by hiking up from the base of Crabtree Falls (three miles) if your vehicle or road conditions are not suitable, or if you want a longer hike. The "Meadows" are now being reclaimed by the forest and are not as open as the name implies. It is, however, a great access point for additional interesting hiking options. From here you can not only hike downhill to the upper cascades of Crabtree Falls, but a half-mile further uphill gets you to the AT. Once you reach the AT, hike east to the Priest (summit) in Priest Wilderness, west if going to Spy Rock, a large rock outcropping with 360-degree views. Use a map if going on the AT, and take the usual precautions for wilderness hiking. Camping is not allowed in the parking area, but there are toilet facilities. You can find several primitive undeveloped sites nearby.

Crabtree Meadows can be reached by turning (right if coming from the Parkway) off VA 56 onto VA 826 which is signed both for Crabtree Meadows and that road, VA 826. The recently improved sign says the road is only suitable for 4WD, however most vehicles can make this drive **IF THE ROAD IS DRY.** Many will find the road intimidating if not in a high clearance vehicle (pickup, SUV, van), and there are a couple of very shallow water crossings that might pose a problem for sedans after heavy rains. Help is a long way away in the event of mechanical failure, and cell coverage is spotty, so plan accordingly. Ignoring false leads, drive 3.7 miles from VA 56 to an obvious parking area (no sign) replete with rest rooms. Park here to hike downhill to Crabtree Falls. Walk or drive (4WD) the road a half-mile further to reach the intersection with the Appalachian Trail.

Access the Priest and Priest Wilderness by continuing on the road from Crabtree Meadows about another half-mile to the crossing with the AT. Go north on the AT about a mile to the summit of the Priest. Turning south on the AT, instead or additionally, takes you in about three miles to Spy Rock. This is ridgeline hiking, with elevation gain and loss in excess of the relatively mild grade the map implies. There are limited views until you climb Spy Rock. The scramble up the rocks doesn't require technical equipment, but rudimentary climbing skills are helpful.

Allow 2 hours round trip to the Priest summit from the upper Crabtree Falls Trailhead. Allow at least 4 hours to hike directly to Spy Rock and back.

Spy Rock can also be reached by a very steep climb from a trailhead with its parking area located to the right of and past the Montebello Fish Hatchery. That road (VA 690 Fish Hatchery Road) intersects VA 56 and is well marked, just before the road to Crabtree Meadows. Hike the old road bed and climb over 1000 vertical feet in just over a mile (steep) to the AT. Turn left at the AT, pass a camping area and ascend the spur trail to Spy Rock for superb views.

MORE SIDE TRIPS FOR THE ADVENTUROUS

Saint Mary's Wilderness has several access points, including two unmarked ones on the Parkway. St. Mary's Falls is a distinctive destination that you can reach by multiple routes. The Mine Bank Trail leaves unheralded through a break in the roadside vegetation across from Fork Mountain Overlook, MP 23. It drops over 1,000 vertical feet in about two miles to reach the St. Mary's Trail. Then a left (westward) turn and another two miles or so takes you to an intersection with a 0.75-mile side trail leading to the falls. This is a considerably longer route to the falls with more elevation gain and loss than the hike from the lower trailhead. Loop hikes also offer a variety of options. From MP 22 the gated Forest Road 162 skirts the wilderness and merges with the Bald Mountain Trail leading eventually to Green Pond and Big Levels. The gate is open seasonally but driving the road is a serious 4WD journey. Often this tread resembles a hiking trail more than a road, which is good for hikers, but not so good for drivers. Trailside laurel frequently brush car doors when driving this road; deceptively mellow track alternates with rugged oil pan-gouging ruts. AAA won't cover this tow. Walk it instead.

The *easiest* hike to the falls requires a short drive from the Parkway. Exit north on VA 56 towards Steeles Tavern, turning right (east) on South Bottom Road, VA 608, which becomes Cold Springs Road. Drive 2.3 miles, to where VA 608 makes a deceptive 90-degree right-hand turn that takes you under a railroad trestle. Less than one-fourth mile after going under the trestle, turn right on Forest Road 41 (St. Mary's Road) whose tiny placard is on the post supporting a stop sign. Proceed about 1.2 miles to the dead end and trailhead to the wilderness area.

The hike is on a gentle grade, often through areas of severe flood damage, courtesy of Hurricane Isabel, whose storm waters ravaged this watershed in 2003. The initial impression is a nagging sense of having chosen poorly because of the residual debris. As you approach the falls, the damage becomes obscure and a tranquil sense of wilderness returns. There are several stream crossings, which in autumn may not even dampen your toes, but which could be tricky following a long wet period or heavy rains. About 45 minutes of steady hiking leads to an intersection signed for the falls. Another three-fourths mile gets you there. There are several back country campsites along the way (some illegal), and water is plentiful. In the drought year of 2007 the lower stretches of the river were dry, likely following a subterranean course; the falls still had an attractive, though diminished, flow. See the image on the preceding spread for reference.

Allow 30 minutes drive each way from the Parkway and 90 minutes hiking time each way to the falls. You will need several additional hours to enjoy the wilderness, photograph along the way, have snacks and hang out. Consider this a half-day excursion.

2

the JOYS of OTTER
CREEK to PEAKS

MP 60 - 86

On Parkway

Otter Creek *and* Lake
James River
Fallingwater Cascades
Peaks of Otter
Sharp Top
Abbott Lake

Off Parkway

Devil's Marbleyard
(James River Face Wilderness)

Natural Bridge

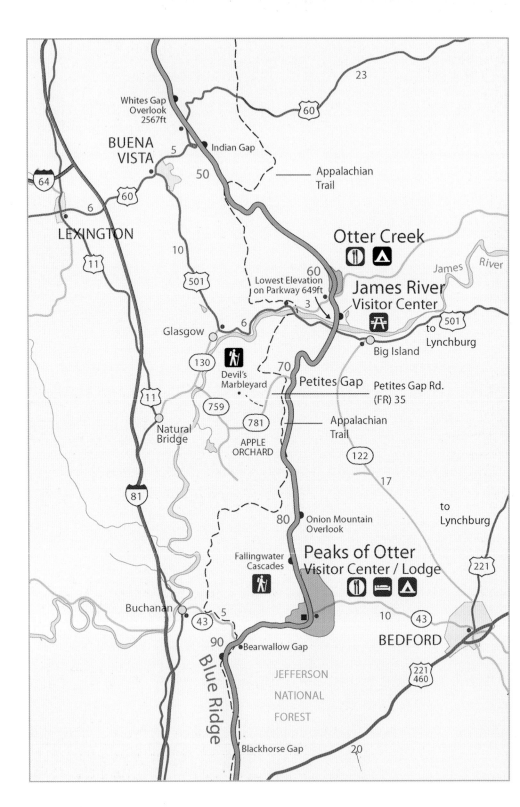

Whites Gap
Overlook
2567ft

Indian Gap

BUENA
VISTA

5

50

Appalachian
Trail

23

60

64

60

6

LEXINGTON

11

10

501

60

Otter Creek

James River

James
River

501

to
Lynchburg

Glasgow

6

3

Lowest Elevation
on Parkway 649ft

Big Island

130

Devil's
Marbleyard

70

Petites Gap

Petites Gap Rd.
(FR) 35

11

759

781

Appalachian
Trail

122

Natural
Bridge

APPLE
ORCHARD

17

to
Lynchburg

81

80

Onion Mountain
Overlook

Peaks of Otter
Visitor Center / Lodge

221

Fallingwater
Cascades

Buchanan

43

5

10

43

BEDFORD

90

Bearwallow Gap

221
460

Blue Ridge

JEFFERSON

NATIONAL

FOREST

Blackhorse Gap

20

Sharp Top's distinctive peak rises above Abbott Lake in early fall. This tranquil scene offers almost endless variations for photographers.

MP	POINT OF INTEREST	FEATURES
60.3	Otter Creek and Lake	Campground, restaurant, hiking
63.6	James River	Visitor Center, hiking, historic features
exit 71	Devil's Marbleyard	Hiking in James River Face Wilderness
exit 71	Natural Bridge	Commercial attraction with multiple services
83.1	Fallingwater Cascades	Short hike to scenic waterfall
86	Peaks of Otter	Major destination with full service lodge, hiking, camping, restaurant, scenic views

MP	LODGING, DINING & GAS	MP	CAMPING
45.6	Buena Vista, US 60 – 5 miles (W)	60.3	Otter Creek
exit 63.9 or 71	Natural Bridge MP 63.9 – U.S. 501, 15 miles (N) or MP 71 – FR 35-VA 781, (exit Petites Gap)	exit 71	Primitive camping along FR 43 / VA 781 towards Devil's Marbleyard – no facilities
86	VA 43 – 9 miles (S) to Bedford	86	Peaks of Otter

MP	LODGING and DINING	MP	RESTAURANT ONLY
86	Peaks of Otter Lodge	60.3	Otter Creek

MP	GASOLINE ONLY	MP	HOSPITAL
exit 63.9	US 501 Big Island – 2 miles (S)	exit 45.6	**Stonewall Jackson Hospital** 540-458-3300 Lexington, VA
		exit 86	**Bedford Memorial Hospital**, 540-586-2441 Bedford, VA

Sharp Top's distinctive reflection is unmistakable in placid Abbott Lake, still as glass.

OVERVIEW

You have many choices to make when planning to enjoy the Otter area. Starting at North Entrance, you can see the first 80 miles comfortably if you only stop for brief leg stretchers and tour the Farm Museum at Humpback Rocks. A long day would even allow a visit to Crabtree Falls and still get you to Peaks of Otter for dinner. You can get to Peaks of Otter directly from I-81 at Buchanan on VA 43, or from Bedford via the same road. You can also day-trip from the towns and cities that flank the Parkway.

You can reach the low country at Otter Creek from Lexington, Buena Vista and Natural Bridge on US 501, if that's more to your liking. Often it's a different season at Peaks of Otter only 2,000 feet higher up.

Leaving Crabtree Falls, the 33-mile drive from the VA 56 intersection, MP 27, to Otter Creek at MP 60, will take the better part of an hour if you don't stop. There are a couple of inviting spots on the way which could slow you down. It's a relaxing drive through forested terrain alternating with open fields, and increasingly broad views as you re-enter the high country.

VA 43 from I-81 is a short, steep, winding mountain road, leading to the Parkway at MP 91, five miles from Peaks of Otter. You can get on the Parkway at Roanoke and make Peaks in 90 minutes or less of leisurely driving.

Winter access via the Parkway is weather dependent but VA route 43, from Buchanan and Bedford, is maintained by the state of Virginia, giving you dependable access.

Spend the night at Peaks of Otter Lodge or campground if you can. This gives you the tranquil hours near dawn and dusk, when Abbott Lake can be still as glass, to enjoy this fabulous place. Early in the morning, Sharp Top's perfect reflection is disturbed only by the ripples made by rising smallmouth bass. Camping and food service are available at Otter Creek and Peaks of Otter. Peaks of Otter Lodge is open year round — reservations are recommended. Call 800-542-5927.

Mountain laurel will bloom through here in late May, and the gorgeous magenta blooms of the Catawba rhododendron, grace higher elevations at the same time, often co-mingling their complementary colors in a delightful transition zone. Early May finds dogwood and red-buds and ground-blooming wildflowers in full splendor. Mid-October finds fall color peaking at the higher elevations with the show continuing until month's end at the lower elevations. The unusually late fall display of 2007 saw color well past mid-November at the lower elevations.

Indian Gap, MP 47.5 (2,098), offers a short 10-15 minute leg-stretcher among huge boulders that are unfortunately marred by graffiti. **Thunder Ridge**, MP 75 (3,485), offers access to the AT and the diminutive Thunder Ridge Wilderness Area. You can take a short stroll, hike on the AT or walk to the overlook perch. It's a convenient drop-off or pick-up point for a longer hike through Virginia's smallest (2,344 acres) federally designated wilderness area. Petites Gap would make a convenient destination for about a 4-mile, one-way hike. The logistics are easier if you have a shuttle driver or a bicycle you can stash.

Plan a short break at Otter Creek, even if it isn't your night's destination. Enjoy the coffee shop for a meal or snack, and browse the gift shop for souvenirs and printed materials. Hiking trails offer short strolls into the hardwood forest and trails also follow the creek and lake. Nearby James River with its visitor center comes up before you have quite gotten your seatbelt adjusted, and is of historic interest. From there you begin the 20-mile ascent to the lofty highlands of Peaks of Otter. Off-Parkway options include wilderness hiking in the adjacent James River Face Wilderness Area, and a touring option to the Natural Bridge, once owned by Thomas Jefferson.

For those bypassing the off-Parkway options, continue driving to MP 83.1 and the parking area for the **Fallingwater Cascades** trail, as well as the longer ascent to Flat Top and Harkening Hill.

Reflections in Otter Lake take on a painterly quality. Be observant! Otters still live here and are sometimes seen when least expected.

The 0.3-mile descent to the top of the cascades is easy going downhill, and moderate on the return. There are about 280 vertical feet to climb spread out over a half-mile.

The Parkway takes you to Peaks of Otter and Abbott Lake three miles further, at MP 86. The inviting coolness of the highlands and the magnificent Abbott Lake scene often trump the lowlands for a place to spend the night. The view of Sharp Top reflecting in the still waters is rivaled by few locations in our entire nation. Non-hikers will find this a great place to "hang out" and soak in the sublime views and clean mountain air. Peaks of Otter is definitely the compelling destination on this Parkway section.

The James River, framed by early spring greenery, presents a tranquil setting for a picnic or a few moments of relaxation.

OTTER CREEK AND LAKE (650)

60.3

🚻 ♿ 🍴 ⛺ 🚶

As the Parkway descends to Otter Creek you will find tranquil wooded scenes along the meandering stream. Spring and fall colors alike delight the senses and photographers will find the color palette appealing. Nearby short hikes offer variety, but more compelling hiking opportunities await in a few miles. If your time is limited, save it for Peaks of Otter. It's all good, but Peaks is the dominator in this neck of the woods.

The coffee shop serves three meals a day, featuring hearty country fare, and the staff is friendly and helpful. My last order of scrambled eggs and bacon would have fed a small scout troop. The gift shop offers souvenir items and a variety of printed materials. The reclusive river otter still calls these waters home and can sometimes be seen swimming in the creek and lake. There are several overlooks along Otter Creek north of the lake, and much of the area can be visually enjoyed from the road. The overlooks offer intimate views rather than sweeping vistas.

Allow 45 - 60 minutes for a meal and shopping, one hour to hike the Otter Lake Trail.

The outlet dam below Otter Lake creates a pleasing roadside cascade.

63.6 James River (649)

The small visitor center offers Parkway information, a picnic area, two short hiking trails and a small museum. The Trail of Trees takes you one-half mile past overlooks of the James River, climbing through a hardwood forest with informational plaques regarding several species of trees in the area. The James River Canal Trail takes you under the bridge on a walkway to a set of locks used when the river was a thoroughfare for commerce in the 19th century. The bridge also serves as the river crossing for the AT. The visitor center is wheelchair accessible.

Allow 30 minutes for the Trail of Trees, 30 - 45 minutes for the Canal Trail.

83.1 Fallingwater Cascades (2,557)

This National Recreation Trail takes you down a moderate trail to the graceful Fallingwater Cascades. It's about 0.3 mile to the first falls and another quarter-mile will take you beyond the last of the cascades. Several spur trails branch off to the base of individual drops. Spring and fall colors offer additional interest. The cascades are recovering from a pine beetle infestation that dropped many large trees into the gorge, reducing, but not eliminating, scenic and photographic enjoyment. The hike back up is a steady but not grueling grade. Return the way you came (shorter), or cross Fallingwater Creek to complete a 1.5 loop hike that kisses the Parkway at Flat Top Overlook, the next overlook along the road. Allow at least an hour to enjoy this hike.

Fallingwater Cascades are a short hike of only moderate difficulty from the Parking Area at MP 83.1. The graceful cascades are well worth the effort.

ABOVE: Rhododendron grace the upper falls.

BELOW: Mountain laurel line the trail to Fallingwater Cascades in late May.

Sunbeams break through the clouds as seen from the Parkway at the "Big Bend," MP 75.5.

Photo Notes

The cascades are in shade until around 9 AM or later, depending on season. Near Memorial Day, mountain laurel and Catawba rhododendron are in peak bloom. Sunbeams breaking through the trees and mist amidst the laurel add a magical accent to the hike. You don't need a camera to enjoy such a scene, but it helps.

Look for sunbeams when the sun is an hour or two off the horizon and the sky is filled with broken clouds.

86   Peaks of Otter (2525)

This is a target-rich environment whether you are a hiker, photographer or just want to relax and enjoy one of the premiere scenic destinations in the country. Peaks of Otter Lodge itself is the attraction for many, offering comfortable accommodations regardless of your planned activities.

The lack of TV in the rooms should be viewed as a plus for those escaping the daily deluge of "too much information," and should prompt you to turn to the

This is one of the best places on the Parkway to watch these develop, but parking is tricky.

natural beauty surrounding this Parkway jewel. The restaurant offers excellent fare, the breakfast buffet is outstanding and the prime rib in the evening is a specialty of the house.

Abbott Lake, named in honor of Parkway architect Stanley Abbott, sits nestled at the base of Sharp Top, a dramatic pyramid-shaped peak a hair under 4000 feet tall. The reflection in the still waters is both dramatic and soothing, and is easily accessible to all. A paved trail follows the shore near the lodge. Anglers can try their luck for smallmouth bass (fishing license required; both VA and NC are honored on Parkway waters).

Across from the visitors center, a nature center offers detailed insights into the critters and plants calling these highlands home. This is also the starting point for the trail to the summit of Sharp Top, and the boarding point for the tram that you can opt to take instead of the steep trail to the peak. The picnic area is a short drive further down VA 43 past the campground.

Polly Woods Ordinary is to the left when you enter the picnic area, and is also accessible from the lake trail. It was one of the first lodgings in these remote mountains, serving travelers with a roof over their heads and basic meals. There

The Johnson Farm hike makes for a pleasant morning outing. Touring the farm can be a brief stop on the way to Harkening Hill or an in depth visit if historical staff are on site.

are several hiking options that follow. You can find area maps at the lodge and visitors center.

Johnson Farm—Harkening Hill Loop: Johnson Farm is a restored homestead previously owned by the John Therone and Mary Johnson family and occupied by their descendants until World War II. The family was self-sufficient on their land, but found a ready market for excess produce and a source of employment for family members at the nearby Mons Hotel, the predecessor to the current Lodge. The Peaks area supported the thriving Mons (Latin for "mountain") community until the 1930s. Tourism was well established in this mountain community until the Great Depression drastically reduced visitation.

The trail departs from a small satellite parking area adjacent to the lodge where it intersects the lake trail. It is about 1.5 miles round-trip to the farm if you don't continue to Harkening Hill, and is suitable for anyone able to walk a gentle grade. Interpretive staff offer demonstrations in the summer months, seasonal crops are planted and harvested, and an interesting glimpse of less complicated times gone by unfolds before you. The Johnsons' descendants still live in the area

Allow at least an hour for the hike, 30 minutes or more to tour the grounds, longer if interpretive programs are running.

Abbott Lake Trail: This mile-long trail circles the lake shore, and is a great way to walk off a meal, or get tuned up for one. It's popular for an early morning stroll, and for cross country skiing if it ever snows again in the Southern Appalachians (sorry, written during a long warm drought). Paved over the portion closest to the lodge, it is wheelchair accessible. It circles past the Polly Woods Ordinary, and follows the shoreline. The easiest access is behind the lodge; park in the lodge parking lot, or as above for the Johnson Farm hike. Alternatively, start your hike from the picnic area if it's crowded.

Sharp Top: Hardy souls (with soles to match) can take the steep 1.4-mile trail to the peak where wait massive boulders, gnarled trees and panoramic views. In late May to early June, Catawba rhododendron and mountain laurel bloom along with late spring wildflowers in this alpine setting. The higher altitude (almost 4,000 feet) at the summit creates conditions normally found much farther north. At the peak are huge rocks, 360 degree views, and a fine view of Abbott Lake below. A shuttle bus runs to the top and back for those not inclined to walk the steep trail to the top; meet at the nature center across the Parkway from the camp store. The tram currently costs eight dollars for a round trip; if it's a slow day you may need to arrange your return time with the driver. You can get tickets at the nearby camp store or from the driver, who may need exact change. The store offers basic camping supplies and ice, but no longer sells gasoline.

PHOTO NOTES

Sharp top sits south of the lodge, getting cross light in early morning or late evening. Full light on the mountain takes about an hour after sunrise, and gives way to shadow in the late afternoon. Clouds will catch light early and late in the day and reflect in the lake if the waters are still. Attractive reed beds and cattails offer foreground interest, and you can frame the peak with various trees along the shore. Maples on the island show intense fall color at their peak, and deer wander through at all hours of the day. Few locations can equal this setting: you can have your camera set up and waiting while you monitor events from the dining room or lounge.

Fantastic rock shapes adorn Sharp Top's summit.

OFF PARKWAY

 exit 71 | **Devil's Marbleyard Natural Bridge**

The Natural Bridge: Now operated privately, this landmark was once owned by Thomas Jefferson. It was one of two early "natural" tourist attractions along with Niagara Falls. It is listed in the National Register of Historic Places and is designated as a National Historic Landmark. George Washington performed one of the original surveys in 1750. Jefferson purchased a tract of land that included this feature and it remained in the family until sold in the 1800s. Today, the Natural Bridge blends a mixture of history and tourism. A re-created Monacan Indian Village offers a glimpse of early Native American life.

The Natural Bridge is a developed commercial attraction with historic interest; natural features include underground caverns and interpretive programs.

The Monacan Indian Nation conducts programs at a recreated 18th century tribal village.

The Natural Bridge itself is an imposing arch 90 feet wide and 215 feet tall with a paved walkway and tranquil stream beneath. Lodging and dining are available on site and nearby.

Access from the Parkway is a continuation of the trek to Devil's Marbleyard described on page 38. You can also get there via US 501 from Glasgow, then VA 130 to Natural Bridge Station and on to the Natural Bridge itself. I-81 is a few short miles away; exits 175, 180, 180-A and 180-B will all get you there.

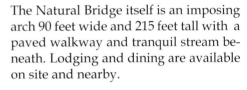

Allow at least two hours to visit the Monacan Village and see the Natural Bridge; shopping and dining options at your discretion.

LEFT: Polly Woods Ordinary sits close to the Lake Trail, and is also accessible from the picnic area.

RIGHT: Sharp Top reflects predawn light in Abbott Lake.

James River Face Wilderness – Devil's Marbleyard Hike

The Devil's Marbleyard is a unique tumble of giant white Antietam quartzite boulders, some the size of automobiles, that flows from the high reaches of Gunter Ridge. If you know where to look, you can see this rocky cascade from many miles away, particularly in the afternoon when it catches the evening sun. There are a few similar fields in Western Virginia, but this is probably the most accessible. Its unique beauty, relative ease of access both by car and foot, and pristine wilderness setting screamed for inclusion in this guide.

The hike is relatively mellow to the base of the formation, passing through second-growth forest, and following the trickling waters of Belfast Creek for a while. The "yard" is several hundred vertical feet in elevation, and a scramble to the summit is a daunting task, not for the faint of heart, or small children. The boulders are for the most part stable, but individual hunks can shift when you put your weight on them, so caution is advised. A landslide is unlikely, but a spill with broken bones is easy to imagine, and the sharper edges could inflict a serious wound. Your view to the west is unspoiled, and afternoon light is your friend whether photographing or enjoying the sights. Sunset here is an option; afterglow in the twilight sky is usually sufficient to find your way back to the car without a flashlight.

Getting There

To find this hidden gem, exit MP 71 at Petites Gap to descend the well-graded Forest Service Road 35 (also named Petites Gap Road, it becomes VA 781 later as you descend) about four miles. When you reach pavement, start looking to your right for the parking area for the Belfast Trail. You will pass other trailheads and primitive camping sites along the way. Cross Elk Creek on a foot bridge, and continue ahead through an old summer camp. Avoid false leads — the Glenwood Horse Trail crosses and conjoins briefly from the right before it branches off to your left. Follow the blue blazes about a mile and a half to the base of the formation, where you can scramble up the huge boulders, or skirt the right side of the formation to reach Gunter Ridge above. Retrace your steps if you came mainly to see the fabulous rock formations, or continue onward to loop back via Gunter Ridge and a section of the Glenwood Horse Trail for an 8-mile outing.

Allow about 15 minutes drive from the Parkway to the trailhead. Plan an hour or so hiking time to the base of the Marbleyard each way. Add an hour to climb to the top of the boulder field, or 20-30 minutes to ascend the trail off to the side, plus time to enjoy the view or photograph.

Continuing on Petites Gap Road, turn right at the intersection with Arnold Valley Road, follow it to the intersection with VA 130, then left on VA 130 about a mile and a half to reach Natural Bridge.

Virginia's
EXPLORE PARK
and
ROANOKE

MP 115 - 121

Explore Park

Roanoke Mountain

the City *of* Roanoke

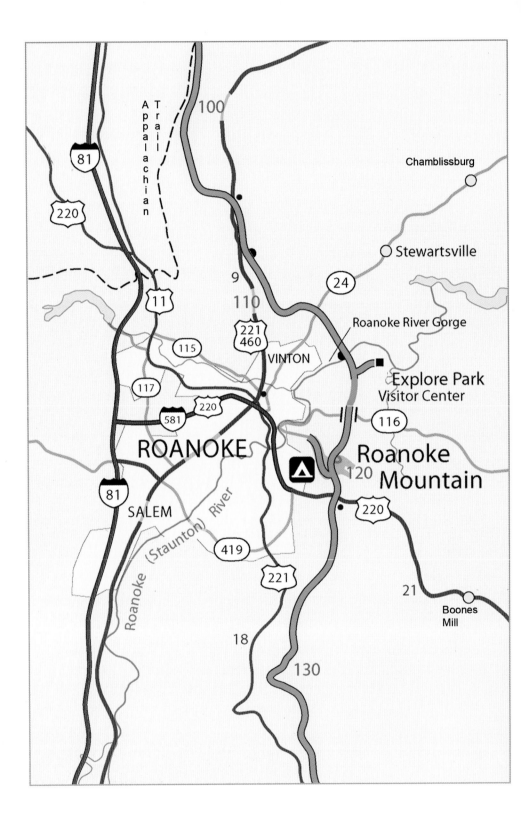

At all seasons, beauty surrounds you on the Parkway, including those "in between" miles that pass twixt one major feature and the next. This composition of redbud leaves and maples is found at the intersection of the Blue Ridge Parkway and the Roanoke River Parkway as it branches off to the Explore Park. "It's all good"!

MP	POINT OF INTEREST	FEATURES	
115	Virginia's Explore Park	Visitor center, living history demonstrations, hiking, biking, canoeing, fishing CHECK FOR CURRENT AVAILABILITY.	
MP	**LODGING**	**MP**	**CAMPING**
121.4	US 220 – west to first exit, then either direction on Franklin Road	120.5	Roanoke Mountain Campground a BRP facility
121.4	Multiple sites along exits 2-5 on U.S. 220 to the west, which becomes I-581		
MP	**RESTAURANTS**		
121.4	Along U.S. 220 in first mile west off the BRP and as above		
MP	**GASOLINE**	**MP**	**HOSPITAL**
121.4	U.S. 220 less than 1 mile west of Parkway	121.4	**Roanoke Memorial Hospital** 540-981-7000 – U.S. 220, west to Franklin Rd. – Call for directions

SPECIAL NOTE

Virginia's Explore Park closed its routine operations at the end of the 2007 season, pending reorganization. The board of directors hopes to finalize arrangements for long-term leasehold improvements and additional construction to expand operations. It is still uncertain at press time when operations will resume. This section is included for the day when the park reopens, and in recognition of the wonderful job the staff has done for the past 21 years. The Parkway Visitor Center remains open.

OVERVIEW

The 1100-acre Explore Park was (is) the compelling feature in this chapter of this guide; its immediate proximity to Roanoke creates many choices and opportunities. Created in 1986 by the General Assembly as part of a public-private partnership, the Park's centerpiece is an outdoor living history museum. The living history demonstrations rival even the well established programs at Williamsburg and Jamestown in quality though not in scope. The Explore Park can easily be visited in a half day or less if the historical venues are your main interest. It's an easy walk, and various options including golf cart shuttles are available to those with disabilities. The Park's attractions don't end there, however. Outdoor recreation opportunities include hiking, 8.5 miles of mountain biking trails (bike rentals available), and river access for fishing, canoeing and kayaking. Check to see what trails and river access points remain open during the reorganization period.

The Roanoke River overlook at MP 114.8 affords an elevated view of the river, and there is a short 10-minute walk to a pedestrian overlook of the river and riverside access for hiking or fishing. The Roanoke Mountain Motor Loop MP 120.3 is a 4-mile drive to the summit of Roanoke Mountain, restricted to vehicles less than 20 feet in length for good reason. A short 10-minute summit trail affords a leg stretcher through the woods. Intimate close up views of the forest make this a worthwhile detour.

Left: The 19th Century Hofauger Farmhouse.

Right: An interior image of a Totero Indian dwelling.

The Mill Mountain spur at MP 120.5 takes you to hiking trails, a Parkway campground, the Mill Mountain Zoo and the Roanoke Star. There is a large overlook at the base of the star where you can watch the sparkling city lights below under the huge neon star overhead. You can descend from the star into Roanoke via Mill Mountain Parkway or return to the Blue Ridge Parkway to enter town via US 220 less than a mile further south.

The city of Roanoke itself offers all the amenities you would expect from a hip major metropolitan area. If you miss the bright lights, internet access or diverse dining options, this is for you. Take the US 220 exit at MP 121.4 north into the city. You will quickly encounter restaurants, grocery stores, and gas stations.

The first major exit, Franklin Road, leads to dining, lodging and shopping. Proceed further into Roanoke to the city center, the Farmers Market, and I-81 if you need major highway access to end your trip. Of course I-81 is also a main point of entry as well. Roanoke's many pleasures are beyond this book's scope.

The 35 miles to Peaks of Otter and 50 miles to Mabry Mill are short enough

drives to enable relaxed exploration of these two wonderful scenic areas while returning for comfortable "metro" evenings. Indeed, Roanoke is almost dead center for the entire Virginia stretch of the Blue Ridge Parkway. You just need to decide your agenda, and how much driving you want to do in one day.

Virginia's

115 Explore Park (950)

Since the exact form that the future Explore Park will take is still unclear, this section is a tribute to what was, and an anticipation of what will be. Follow the spur road to the central Parkway Visitor Center which plans to remain in operation throughout the transition. Park here and get up-to-date information on currently available activities.

Your walking tour would begin here through the Arthur Taubman Welcome Center, down the Salem Turnpike to the 17th century era Totero Indian Village. First contact with this tribe dates to the late 1600s; the recreation is nearly devoid of European influence. Authentic techniques were used to reconstruct the village.

Follow the Salem Turnpike to the Augusta County Frontier Fort, a replica of frontier times, then under threat of raids in various wars including the French and Indian War of 1756-1763. Inside the confines of the stockade, staff members recreate daily life on the frontier.

The next demonstration brings you closer to familiar times with the Hofauger Farmstead and surrounding structures, moved here for the re-creation of an intact community replete with grist mill. The loop trail ends soon after at a butterfly garden and picnic pavilion. If you need a shuttle back to the parking area, ask a staff member to radio for a golf cart, otherwise it's an easy walk.

Hiking trails include the Society of American Foresters Trail. Less than three fourths of a mile in length. Allow an hour to soak in the educational features of the trail. Other options include the River Walk (stream side), Back Creek and Turkey Scratch trails. Mountain biking enthusiasts will find both beginner and expert level trails in the Park. There is river access for boating (self-propelled, no motors) and fishing. Photographers will enjoy the period structures and interpretive staff, reflections in the Roanoke River and the many hues and moods the forest offers.

CLOCKWISE FROM LEFT, OPPOSITE PAGE: 1. Period historical staff at the Frontier Fort. 2. Historian Eddie Goode works an 18th century wood lathe. 3. Firewood stacked on the porch. 4. Interior detail at Hofauger Farmstead. BELOW: A Monet-like reflection in the placid waters of the Roanoke River.

Photo Notes

Photographing these structures, as well as most forest scenes, gives more pleasing images in overcast or cloudy conditions. Soft diffused light is free of harsh shadows and is perfect for this type of imaging. Often you get there in less than ideal conditions. Being aware of local options can make the difference between ho-hum and great photos.

Interior photography is less dependent on time of day or outside conditions, so the weather doesn't matter so much. The Roanoke River reflects patterns from its far (eastern) shore in mid-afternoon if you have sunny conditions (you will be standing on the western shore). These reflections make great subjects on a sunny day when harsh shadows are otherwise a problem.

In late afternoon, as long shadows creep up the far bank, you will lose the highest quality reflections. Then it's a good time to photograph the pioneer cabins in softer light. In such deeply shaded conditions, use the automatic white balance setting on your digital camera to counteract the blue cast imparted by the overhead sky.

A tranquil forest scene waits at the end of the Roanoke Mountain Scenic Loop Road. Such beauty is all around you on the Parkway if you take the time to look.

4

MABRY MILL
and
ROCKY KNOB

MP 167 - 190

ROCK CASTLE GORGE TRAIL
MABRY MILL
GROUNDHOG MOUNTAIN
PUCKETT CABIN

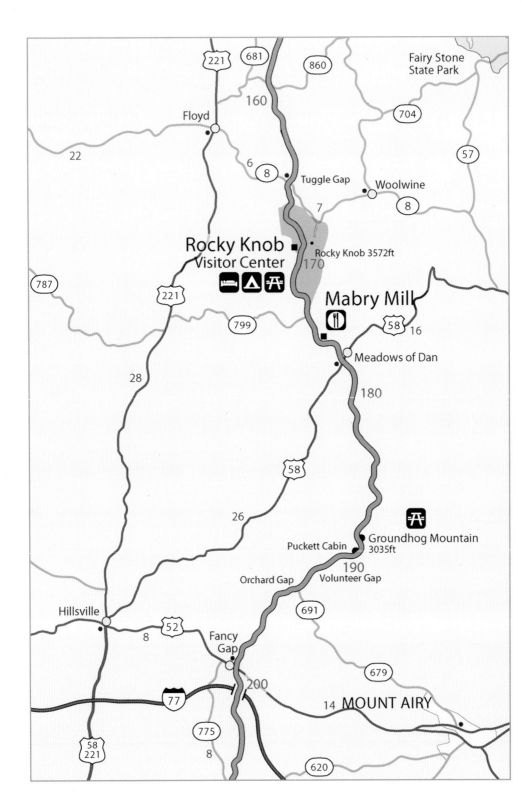

Mabry Mill has weathered many seasons through the years since Ed Mabry first turned a wheel here. Spring brings the blooming sarvis tree, summer the magenta blooms of the Catawba rhododendron, autumn a riot of color, and winter an icy grip.

MP	POINT OF INTEREST	FEATURES
167-169	Rocky Knob Recreation Area	Rock Castle Gorge hike, campground
176.2	Mabry Mill	Historic and interpretive site
180.5	Mayberry Country Store	Nostalgia
188.8	Groundhog Mountain	Picnic area, interpretive displays
189.9	Puckett Cabin	Historic site

MP	LODGING AND DINING	MP	CAMPING
165.3	Tuggle Gap, and six miles west in Floyd, VA on VA 8	168	Rocky Knob Campground, a BRP facility
174.1	Rocky Knob Housekeeping Cabins	177.7	Meadows of Dan (commercial)
177.7	Meadows of Dan	199.4	Fancy Gap (commercial)
199.4	Fancy Gap		

MP	GASOLINE	MP	HOSPITAL
165.3	Tuggle Gap, and six miles west in Floyd, VA on VA 8	165.3	**Montgomery Regional Hospital** Floyd, VA, take VA 8, six miles west of BRP 540-953-5122
177.7	Meadows of Dan	199.4	**Northern Hospital of Surry County** Mt. Airy, NC – 14 miles east on U.S. 52 336-719-7000
193.7	Orchard Gap	MP	RESTAURANT ONLY
199.4	Fancy Gap	176.2	Mabry MIll

The trail follows Rock Castle Creek for several miles, and is a wildflower lover's delight in late April and early May.

OVERVIEW

Travelers following the Parkway start to finish will find a bit over a one hour drive nonstop from Roanoke to the Rocky Knob area. The tables on page 52 list the on-or-near Parkway lodging options. This section of the Parkway is accessible from multiple other approaches, with several roads crossing from I-81, which mostly parallels the Parkway to the north and west. VA 8 from Christiansburg runs through Floyd to reach the Parkway in about 30 miles. I-77 departs I-81 about eight miles north of Wytheville, VA, to reach the Blue Ridge Parkway at Fancy Gap near the 200 milepost. Mount Airy is a few miles east (south, really — there's that highway numbering convention thing) of Fancy Gap on US 52. The drive from Roanoke is filled with subtle charms, but this part of Virginia lacks the dramatic scenes that more mountainous Parkway sections are endowed with. Relax and enjoy the ride — it's why you came!

Smart View Recreation Area at MP 154.5 provides a break from driving at the historic Trail Cabin, perched on the hillside, offering sweeping views of the foothills below. This is one of the few historic structures in its original location on the Parkway. It was just the sort of picturesque cabin that Parkway developers hoped to preserve, along with its history. You will find a picnic area, rest rooms and a hiking trail that offers a total loop of three miles, with shortcut options that can reduce the distance. Rock Castle Gorge is little more than 15 miles farther south, and has more interesting and varied hiking options. Though interesting enough, Smart View is more of a rest break or picnic stop, than a destination.

Matthews Cabin was built in 1869 in the nearby Mount Lebanon community and was moved to its current site in 1956 to supplement the Mabry Mill's interpretive site.

Rocky Knob (3,300) Recreation Area

 167-9

This is the more "nature-oriented" of the two nearly adjacent points of interest, the other being of course Mabry Mill. Here at Rocky Knob you will find a campground, hiking trails, a back country campsite and housekeeping cabins, with Mabry being just a few miles distant. This area is about 3,500 acres in size, and is one of a few areas where Parkway lands constitute more than a roadside right of way.

Multiple hiking options await, including the 10.6-mile Rock Castle Gorge Trail. Overnight backcountry camping requires a free permit, obtainable at the visitor center. The hike is easily broken up into sections, depending on your goals and ambitions. A short detour from the Parkway south on VA 8 at Tuggle Gap brings you to a lower trailhead to access Rock Castle Creek (so named for the large quartzite crystals found in the area, like miniature "rock castles").

If you are staying in the campground, there are several nearby dining options if you want a break from kitchen duty.

Mabry Mill (2,855)

176.2

Mabry Mill is an icon. The mill has been photographed often enough to make George Eastman smile in his grave, and has even been (mis) represented as being in other counties and states. It is full of history, although the current site has been restored beyond its original configuration. Addition of the reflecting pond makes for a more photogenic scene, and is not out of character. Other structures were brought in, and Ed Mabry's sideboard house is no longer there. The current display is in keeping with a late 1800s or early 1900s era in mountain history and is totally enchanting. Most visitors look at the mill, snap a few pics, visit the gift shop, maybe the restaurant and then go on their way. The half-mile Mountain Industry Trail gives you a more in depth tour.

Living history displays and Sunday afternoon music offer variety and a great reason to extend your visit. The grist mill is in operation on weekends, with various other demonstrations through the week. An overflow parking area with its own comfort station lies a few hundred yards north of the mill, and connects to the Mountain Industry Trail which leads you to the mill in less than a quarter mile. Tour buses frequently stop here; however, their time is usually brief, so just wait for the crowd to thin down a bit if there are too many folks for you.

Allow 30 minutes to 2-3 hours.

RIGHT: A collection of old mill stones. Closer study reveals the intricate patterns of gears and grinding surfaces.

BELOW: Mountain laurel blooms at the Mabry Mill in late May and early June.

MAYBERRY TRADING POST
MP 180

OK — you almost drove right by it — but, if you look carefully, you can see it from the road. The name Mayberry became famous on the Andy Griffith Show. Even if you are too young to have seen it in prime time, it's still in reruns. Here it is — a slice of Americana that generations grew up with. Story has it that Andy Griffith's grandfather was a regular customer at this Mayberry country store. Mr. Griffith himself, grew up in nearby Mt. Airy, upon which the TV town was supposedly modeled. The goings-on in these communities no doubt figured into many episodes, as did the overall flavor of life in a small rural community. The store today carries basic staples, local crafts, produce and a heaping dose of nostalgia and hospitality. Drop in for a visit.

RIGHT: Puckett Cabin

BELOW: Snake rail fencing and the lookout tower at Groundhog Mountain.

 188.8 Groundhog (3,030) Mountain 🚻🏕♿

This picnic area offers another rest stop, picnic area and a self service interpretive site. A main feature is the various fencing types used in the southern Appalachians. The snake rail (also known as the Virginia split rail) fence is among the most picturesque and most commonly seen on the Parkway.

 189.9 Puckett Cabin (2,848)

This roadside cabin was once the home of Aunt Orelena Puckett, a famous midwife who was credited with hundreds, perhaps over a thousand deliveries in her career, without losing a patient. The site and structure are original.

Allow a few minutes each.

ROCK CASTLE GORGE HIKING

The loop trail through the gorge and its ascent and descent from the high crest of the Blue Ridge gets a strenuous rating due to the significant and often rather abrupt elevation changes. Being a loop trail, it can be broken down into much easier segments quite easily. Those wanting scenic views can make shorter hikes staying near the spine of the Blue Ridge, avoiding the stress and strain on various body parts that the ascent and descent puts one through. The trail is never very far from the Parkway; park at any overlook, the campground, or the visitor center for however long a walk you like. Maps are available at the visitor center and campground, and there is a large wooden display showing the map as well. Return the way you came, stash a bike, or have a friend pick you up.

In late April and early May, the wildflower display along Rock Castle Creek trumps the high ridge for hiking splendor. All the usual southern Appalachian beauties are found here, and in glorious profusion — over 200 species by one count. Rock Castle Creek has higher flows in the spring making for more pleasing views and photos. To top it all, there is a lower entry that rates easy and mellow on the grunt and sweat scale.

The gently graded trail follows the creek for almost three miles, crossing three times on sturdy bridges. Tear off as much as you feel like before retracing your steps or, if you have a shuttle, continue on to climb out of the gorge to the ridge line and Parkway above. Dedicated hikers can tromp the entire 10.6- mile distance with the choices being to begin or end with a steep climb of some 1,700 vertical feet. This choice dictates the starting point. The lower trail head (directions below) allows a descent at the end, or a shorter mellow out and back jaunt. Along the way, please respect the privacy of the residents of Austin House, a privately owned residence which is still a family in-holding within the Gorge. Built in 1916, it was the proud centerpiece of a once thriving community of 30 families living here.

GETTING THERE

Follow VA 8 south from Tuggle Gap, for 3.2 miles to the first intersection from the right. This is CCC Camp Lane, SR 605, which leads in about 0.6 miles to the end of the road and the trailhead for the Rock Castle Gorge. When you reach the sign that says "end state maintenance," the parking area is less than a hundred yards ahead. Park, and cross the shallow creek to begin your hike. The turn-off from VA 8 does not indicate that the road is heading to Parkway property. This stretch of VA 8 affords a wonderful "squirrel's-eye" view of the forest interior. In mid-to-late October this drive would be outrageously colorful. Several small turnouts afford the opportunity to safely stop to soak it all in.

LEFT: Rock Castle Creek in early May, graced by a spring bouquet.

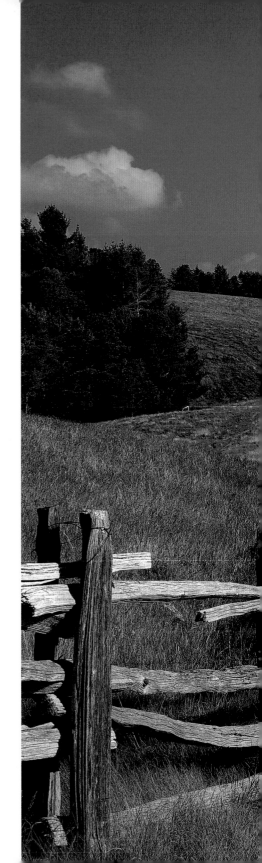

5

DOUGHTON PARK

BLUE RIDGE
MUSIC CENTER

CUMBERLAND KNOB

BRINEGAR CABIN

BLUFF MOUNTAIN TRAIL

MP 200 - 245

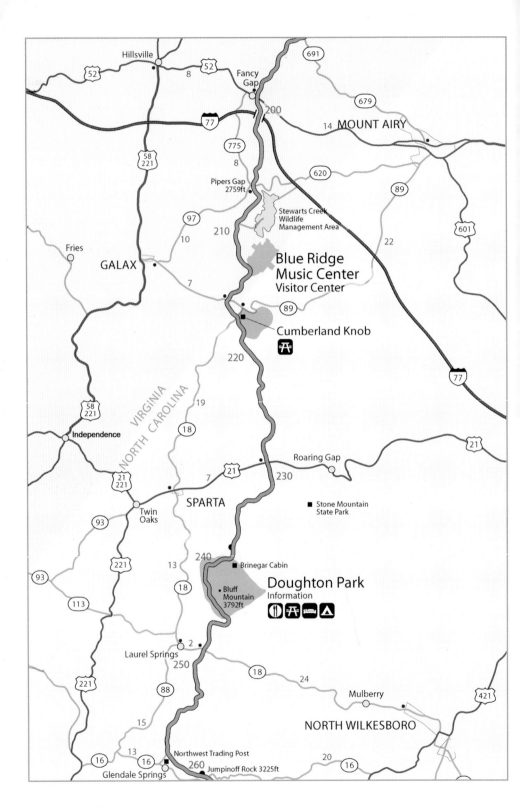

Attractive post and rail fence rows line fields and roadways at Doughton Park.

MP	POINT OF INTEREST	FEATURES	
213.3	Blue Ridge Music Center	Visitor center, museum, live performances, hiking trails	
217.9	Cumberland Knob	Picnic area, views	
238.5	Brinegar Cabin	Historic structures, interpretive programs	
238.6 to 244.8	Doughton Park	Camping, hiking, coffee shop, Bluffs Lodge, information	
MP	**LODGING AND DINING**	**MP**	**CAMPING**
215.8	VA 89 — Galax, 7 miles north	238.6	Doughton Park Campground
229.7	U.S. 21 — Roaring Gap 4 miles south — Sparta 7 miles north		
238.6	Bluffs Lodge, Doughton Park		
MP	**GASOLINE**	**MP**	**HOSPITAL**
215.8	VA 89 — Galax, 7 miles north	215.8	VA 89 — **Twin County Regional Hospital** Galax, 7 miles north 276-236-8181
229.7	U.S. 21 — Roaring Gap, 4 miles south — Sparta, 7 miles north	229.7	U.S. 21 — **Allegheny Memorial** Sparta 7 miles (N) 336-372-5511

Spring brings infinite shades of green to the rolling hills near Cumberland Knob, and maples add a splash of color. This pastoral scene hasn't fallen victim to the satellite dish yet.

OVERVIEW

The Parkway leaves the historical sites at Mabry Mill and Puckett Cabin and meanders its way through the Virginia countryside to its rendezvous with the Blue Ridge Music Center, Cumberland Gap, and the 6,000-acre Parkway Recreation Area at Doughton Park. There is a relative scarcity of nearby services through this stretch; those available to you near Fancy Gap are detailed in the preceding chapter. After leaving Fancy Gap, the small communities of Galax, Sparta and Roaring Gap offer the closest services. This section of Parkway rolls through the now-familiar rural Virginia countryside in this higher plateau region of Virginia with little notice as you enter North Carolina. Here the scenes are vignettes of modern rural life; as you approach Doughton Park unspoiled vistas begin to unfold. The rural landscape has changed through the years since the first shovel was turned on the Parkway, though the quaintness that Parkway designers sought to preserve had, for the most part, already vanished from the contemporary scene before the Parkway was built.

The Blue Ridge Music Center, MP 213.3, a cooperative venture between the National Park Service and the National Council for the Traditional Arts, is a relative newcomer to the Parkway. This has been music country for many years, and nearby Galax has hosted the annual Old Fiddler's Convention since August 1935, attracting many thousands of musicians and listeners. The summer concerts at the Music Center likewise attract talent and music lovers from miles away. The visitor center has recently

The Blue Ridge Music Center hosts a fascinating museum display detailing the area's musical history with many memorabilia and instruments. There is almost always live music on site.

been moved here from nearby Cumberland Knob.

Cumberland Knob: September 11, 1935 — the first shovel of dirt is turned near MP 217.5. The following year saw completion of the first short section nearby. Two short hiking trails offer leg stretching options; there is a picnic area and the views are pleasing. Its history alone makes it worthy of a stop.

This section of the guidebook ends with the great expanse of Doughton Park. With its photogenic split rail fences, nowhere is the road itself more attractive. This 6,000 acre preserve is one of two places where overnight backcountry camping is possible. An extensive trail system, coffee shop, overnight lodging at the Bluffs Lodge, a campground and nearby historic Brinegar Cabin offer something for almost everyone. Bluffs Lodge is strategically located to give

visitors a convenient lodging option in this otherwise remote section. Gas is no longer available at Doughton or any other Parkway location.

213.3 Blue Ridge Music Center

This recent addition to the Parkway adds depth to its interpretive mission. Here is a focal point for presentation of traditional music styles whose roots run deep in these mountains and valleys. Having a place to perform is key to keeping these musical traditions alive. Artists whose passion must be balanced with the more mundane tasks of earning a living perform here, as well as full- time professional musicians. Country, bluegrass and spiritual genres meld and overlap here. You will find a modern visitor center, museum-quality gallery, outdoor concert area and gift shop.

Brinegar Cabin as seen looking up from the spring house

There are short hiking trails, though it's hard to imagine going for a walk here when live music is playing—which, by the way, is most of the time. When there isn't a concert as such going on, there are usually visiting or staff musicians performing impromptu sets in the adjacent breezeway. Pull up a chair, listen, and in between songs, take an opportunity to chat with the performer.

Allow 30 minutes to hours and hours.

217.5 Cumberland Knob (2,885)

This is where it all started, but the area seems to be sinking into obscurity. The visitor center moved to the nearby Blue Ridge Music Center, and Doughton Park are but a short 20 miles away.

Mrs. Brinegar preserved food weeks in advance to get through the cold barren months. The winter diet followed a sequence dictated by preservation methods. Root vegetables went into (what else,) the root cellar. When they were getting a bit rank around the end of February, the family would move on to pickled foods, then dried, in hopes of stretching things until the new spring crops came in. Meats were salted or smoked, and wild game sometimes supplemented the menu. Above, in the original root cellar-granary is a sampling of bloody butcher corn, broom corn (sorghum), dried apples and beans. An original cider press sits in the corner. Interpretive staff maintain the cabin and grow seasonal crops in the same fashion as the Brinegars did years ago.

A hiker seems to be holding up a leaning tree (or is it the other way around?) on a grassy knoll at Doughton Park. Overhead a crescent moon dots a clear spring sky.

A picnic area, loop trail and elevated views offer options, but are overshadowed by nearby attractions.

238.5 Brinegar Cabin (3,508)

One of the Parkway's best interpretive sites, when staff are here presenting a demonstration or expounding on Brinegar family history, the cabins and gardens come to life. Here the daily routines of a self-sufficient family in these rural and sometimes isolated mountain communities are preserved. A traditional garden is planted each season.

Allow 15 minutes to an hour or two, depending on presence of interpretive staff.

241 Doughton Park (3,385)

Originally known as the Bluffs, the lodge today retains that name. In 1951 the area was renamed in honor of Robert Doughton, longtime North Carolina Congressman, staunch Parkway supporter and advocate. His voice and support were key in gaining initial approval for the Parkway project. A campground offers overnight options for those so equipped, as an alternative to the Bluffs Lodge. The coffee shop offers basic fare, but is not open late. Thirty miles of hiking trails crisscross the area, and one (Bluff Mountain Trail) parallels the Parkway itself, often hidden from view. You will see most of Doughton Park from on high unless you specifically seek out the Basin Cove trails.

Across from the coffee shop and visitor center, the access road forks to the left to Bluffs Lodge, and the parking area for Wildcat Rocks and Fodderstack Trail, and to the right to the picnic area and trails. Large rhododendron bushes line the roadside.

At Wildcat Rocks parking area, stone steps climb to an overlook looking down to Basin Cove and Caudill Cabin, 1,500 vertical feet below. After the cabin was occupied intermittently for several years, the Caudills relocated downstream closer to other families in the Basin Cove community. Disaster struck in 1916 in the form of unprecedented flooding. Among others, the flood waters killed young Alice Caudill, who being pregnant, had difficulty evacuating. The cabin, being further upstream, ironically escaped damage. The interpretive staff at Brinegar Cabin keep this and many other tales alive. Basin Cove and Caudill Cabin are accessible by trail from a lower entry.

BLUFF MOUNTAIN TRAIL

Alligator Back Overlook, MP 242.4 is a convenient starting point for the Bluff Mountain Trail which ascends to the east, climbing switchbacks through rhododendron- and laurel-lined tunnels to the summit of Bluff Mountain above. As you near the summit, various social trails lead off, however the main thread is easy enough to follow. The summit area is rather indistinct, but rocky outcrops offer views to the west and the setting sun. You can easily reach this same area from the apex of the picnic area's parking loop. Trail signs direct you to this and the Bluff Ridge Trail (which descends steeply to Basin Cove after a ridge line traverse) so don't be confused by the similar names. The Bluff Mountain Trail follows the picnic area access road to the north towards the lodge, coffee shop, and on to Brinegar Cabin. Hiking north (back towards the Parkway) from the picnic area you will soon (in about 400 yards) reach gorgeous high knolls crowned by stately giant oaks. Sadly, recent hurricanes have taken most of those. These exposed knobs have an expansive, alpine feel to them, that is truly refreshing. This short walk from the picnic area is well worth your time, even if you are not a hiker. The tread is gentle and boots are optional. The North Carolina Mountains-to-Sea Trail follows the Bluff Mountain Trail here, and is blazed white. The Bluff Mountain Trail follows the Parkway south a little over two miles before descending Flat Rock Ridge Trail to Basin Cove below. The Mountains-to-Sea Trail follows the Parkway south towards Boone and Blowing Rock and north to Devil's Garden Overlook, MP 235.7 before turning towards Stone Mountain State Park.

RIGHT: Evening light from the summit of Bluff Mountain.

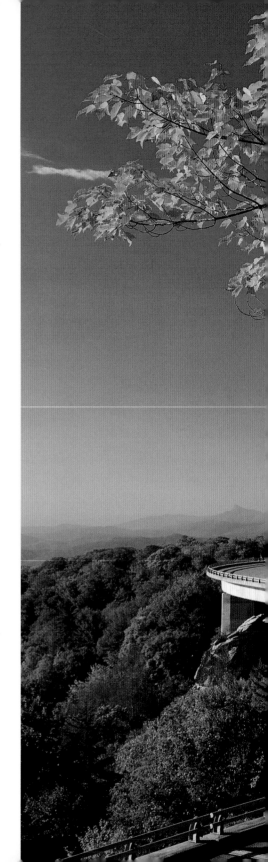

6

GRANDFATHER
BLOWING ROCK

E.B. JEFFRESS PARK
BLOWING ROCK, N.C.
BASS LAKE
MOSES CONE PARK
PRICE PARK
TANAWHA TRAIL
ROUGH RIDGE
LINN COVE VIADUCT
BEACON HEIGHTS
GRANDFATHER MTN.

MP 271 - 305

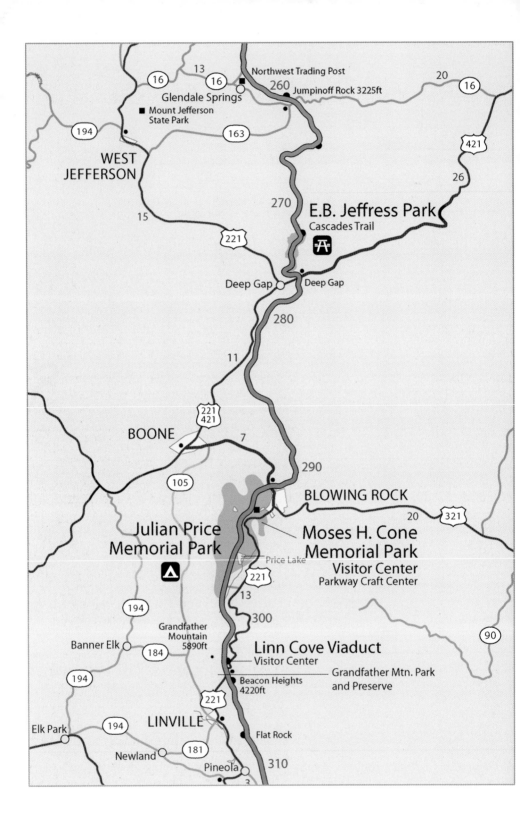

The Parkway winds its way towards Blowing Rock as seen from Rough Ridge.

MP	POINT OF INTEREST	FEATURES
258.6	Northwest Trading Post	Crafts, gift shop, snacks
271.9	E.B. Jeffress Park	Picnic area, hiking, a waterfall, historic cabins
291.9	Boone & Blowing Rock – exit U.S. 221	Lodging, dining, shopping
294	Cone Park & Flat Top Manor	Cone Manor, crafts, hiking
294.6	Bass Lake, exit U.S. 221	Scenery, hiking, photography
296.7	Price Park, Price Lake picnic area and campground	Canoeing, fishing, hiking, camping, picnic area
300	Boone Fork Overlook	Hiking trailhead, backcountry camping
302.8	Rough Ridge Overlook	Hiking trailhead
304	Yonahlossee Overlook	Park to walk to Linn Cove Viaduct
304.4	Linn Cove Visitor Center	Visitor Center, walk to Linn Cove Viaduct
305	Beacon Heights	Short hike to spectacular views, access Tanawha Trail
exit 305	Grandfather Mountain Preserve 1 mile south on U.S. 221	Private nature preserve, multiple features, views, hiking, wildlife habitat enclosures

MP	LODGING, DINING & GAS	MP	CAMPING
258.6	Glendale Springs – exit BRP at NW Trading Post (W) to NC 16	296.7	Price Park, a BRP campground
291.9	Boone & Blowing Rock – exit U.S. 221	**MP**	**HOSPITALS**
294.6	U.S. 221 to Blowing Rock	exit 291.9	Boone, N.C. – **Watauga Medical Center** 800-443-7385
305	U.S. 221 (S) to Linville; also then NC 105 → 184 (W) to Banner Elk		

The Parkway is never far away. Here the road is visible from the boardwalk on Rough Ridge, about a 10-15 minute walk from your car. Rhododendron accent the scene in late May and early June. The preceding page features the same scene in early October.

OVERVIEW

OK folks — let's head to the high country! Parkway through-trippers by now have seen a variety of topography from the rugged Virginia highlands to the banks of the James River and everything in between. Off-Parkway access from either the I-81 or I-40 corridor gives almost endless options — any basic map will get you here. The journey to the heart of the North Carolina mountains lies ahead. The Parkway winds peacefully through farmland and wooded hillsides for about 40 miles with distant views and close-in modern pastoral scenes. You will soon reach the Northwest Trading Post, MP 258.6, with its visitor center and gift shop. The Trading Post features locally crafted wares from surrounding counties and offers snacks, rest rooms and picnicking.

The Parkway curves on past the 600 acre E.B. Jeffress Park at MP 271.9, so named in honor of the North Carolina state highway commissioner who played key roles, both in securing the present Parkway route through North Carolina, and keeping access toll free. Here you will find hiking trails, a waterfall, historic buildings, rest rooms, a water fountain and a picnic area. Twenty miles further down the road brings you to the U.S. 221 crossroads at MP 291.9, with exits to Boone and the high country resort village of Blowing Rock. Blowing Rock has been a resort center for many years and makes a wonderful base from which to explore this section of the Parkway. Those wishing to hold on to their hard-earned cash a bit longer (like me) can camp at nearby Parkway facility Price Lake Campground and still enjoy the town's many amenities. While Blowing Rock can be pricey, there are many moderate dining and lodging options, and many shopping opportunities. This is a target-rich area, loaded with hiking and scenic attractions, including Flat Top Manor at Cone Estate, Bass Lake, and Linn Cove Viaduct. Grandfather Mountain, at 5,964 feet elevation, dominates the to-

The Cascades on Falls Creek are accessible from a gentle 1-mile loop trail. As with most waterfalls, they photograph better on cloudy days or when in shade early and late in the day.

pography, and is the highest peak in the Blue Ridge mountain range. Technically speaking the peaks above 6,000 are in the Black Mountains and other sub-ranges further along to the south. Many hiking trails tread the shoulders and spine of this rugged peak, some on the privately owned Grandfather Mountain property. In one way or another, the mountain affects most things on this section of the Parkway, from scenery to weather.

Grandfather Mountain is more than just a mountain, it is also the name of a privately owned preserve, THE mountain itself. It operates as a nature-oriented destination, much of which is held in trust by the Nature Conservancy. An entrance fee is charged, which includes hiking privileges on the several trails that are accessible from Parkway trailheads at Boone Fork Overlook, MP 300. This UNESCO-designated International Biosphere Preserve is most easily accessible by car from U.S. 221, one mile south of the Parkway exit at MP 305.

Services are plentiful on this stretch after you leave Doughton Park with most ev-

erything a traveler might need in Blowing Rock or nearby Boone. Near Grandfather Mountain, exiting on U.S. 221, the resort towns of Linville and Banner Elk provide additional options. Banner Elk hosts two ski areas as well for winter fun options.

271.9 E.B. Jeffress Park (3,657) 🚻 🎪 ♿ 🚶

This 600-acre park hosts hiking trails, including the short Cascades Nature Trail which leads to an intimate overlook at (what else?) the Cascades, an attractive waterfall on Falls Creek plunging from the escarpment. Falls Creek may seem quite low as you hike along, but the Cascades will have adequate flow to be appealing and photogenic. This one-mile long loop trail starts near the restrooms to the left of the parking area and follows a gentle grade to the falls. There is little time savings to be had from an "out and back" route, so consider the whole loop for variety. As with most waterfalls in the southern mountains, a thin film of clear algae grows on the rocks, making them

This large red maple tree has provided the shade for many a sermon through the years. It now stands guard over the Jesse Brown Cabin and the nearby Cool Springs Baptist Church. The spring house is a short walk behind this vantage point.

quite slick and incredibly dangerous to walk on. The Cascades have claimed lives before; don't add to the body count. Stay behind the guard rail.

Allow 45 minutes to an hour to see the Cascades, 10-15 minutes for Jesse Brown Cabin, longer if photographing.

Jesse Brown Cabin, (MP 272.6) is a short .75 miles down the road, close enough to hike if you are so inclined. Unofficial roadside parking is commonly used; please don't tear up the turf in wet weather. Originally built around 1840, this cabin was moved twice before reaching its present location in 1905 to be closer to a water source. The Cool Springs Baptist Church was also relocated close by. References mention the large red maple that frames the cabin as having been the site of outdoor preaching years ago. The cabin is quite photogenic, and the enclave has historic interest. The roadside berm is rather steep, a bit dicey for wheelchairs

The well-surfaced Bass Lake Trail is truly a walk in the park. Stately maples add intense color here in early October. They tend to change color in the first week of the month, a bit earlier than on the surrounding Parkway.

unless with a burley assistant; the picnic area is handicapped accessible.

294	Moses Cone Memorial Park	

This 3,600 acre estate was donated to the Parkway following Bertha Cone's, (in-

Flat Top Manor recalls the grandeur of grand estate living, shared through the generosity of Moses Cone's estate.

dustrialist Moses Cone's widow) death in 1947. North Carolina's "denim king," Moses Cone made a large fortune in the textile industry, and then moved to this site to pursue a more peaceful lifestyle. Flat Top Manor, also simply known as Cone Manor, is the most famous attraction, a 13,000-square-foot mansion overlooking Bass Lake far below. Twenty seven miles of carriage (now hiking) trails wind through the estate. The manor houses the Parkway Craft Center, one of five Southern Highland Craft Guild locations. It is a MUST-SEE stop.

Detailing the extensive trail system is beyond the scope of this book; however you will find trail guides at the visitor center to help you explore the area. Winter visitors fortunate enough to arrive after a snow storm will find excellent cross country skiing options here.

Bass Lake is an easily reached scenic option whose shoreline trail is wheelchair accessible. This MUST-SEE picturesque lake is lined by stately maples, and has a wonderful view of the mansion on the hillside far above. This is a stroll, not a hike, but what a stroll. It just doesn't get any better than this and it's wheelchair accessible with some assistance. The lake trail connects to an extensive system of former carriage trails, and you can even hike up to the mansion if you wish. Photographers can amuse themselves for hours between reflections in the lake, views of the manor and the maple lined paths.

The parking area is accessible by exiting onto U.S. 221 at MP 294.6 just 0.5 miles south of the Cone Manor entrance. Drive back towards Blowing Rock approximately one mile to the paved entryway. An alternate entry is just beyond on U.S.

Allow a few minutes to an hour to see or stroll around Bass Lake. For Cone Manor, allow 30 minutes to an hour, more if shopping or photographing.

 Price Lake (3,400)

This 4300-acre park was donated to the National Park Service as a public recreation area by Jefferson Pilot Standard Life Insurance Company in memory of its president, Julian Price, who was killed in an automobile crash. The 47-acre Price Lake is the visual centerpiece of Price Park which also sports a large picnic area, the Parkway's largest campground and several trails, including one that circumnavigates the lake. This is a fabulous spot to rent a canoe (if you didn't bring your own) and have a splendid paddle on Price Lake beneath the looming brow of Grandfather Mountain. The lake has an eager fish population — eager to make your day. Remember a valid fishing license is required. Parkway waters honor the Virginia license as well. The picnic area is a day-use area opposite the Lake. The trailhead for the Boone Fork Trail is just behind the rest rooms shortly after you enter the picnic area on your left.

The Boone Fork Trail offers a five-mile loop following the cascades of the lower stretch of Boone Fork (named for Daniel's nephew Jesse) with the 25-foot Boone Fork Falls offering a visual highlight in wet weather. Return the way you came for maximum creek-side hiking, or complete the loop turning left at the Bee Tee Creek junction, and loop back through the campground and the northern terminus of the Tanawha Trail.

Rocking chairs line the porch at Flat Top Manor, giving views to Bass Lake and Blowing Rock below. The pristine views that the Cones enjoyed are now dotted with various developments

 Photo Notes

Bass Lake photographs well in the morning when the maple lined shore reflects brilliant colors onto the still waters. Reflections are more intense when they are in shade with the light hitting the reflecting object. You can photograph Cone Manor from the farther sides of the lake looking back towards the parking area. Cone Manor also receives morning light, and the chairs lined up on the porch evoke feelings of prosperity. Get there early, it gets crowded by mid-morning. Check with staff about any current restrictions on photography at the house itself.

221, which affords access if the first entry is closed because of snow. Bass Lake is a popular place to cross country ski in the winter, if the snow elves are obliging and there are enough hills adjacent for the kids to sled.

RIGHT: Canoeists enjoy a bit of fishing on a crisp fall day on Price Lake. Catch and release fishing is encouraged, but not mandated by law. Boat rentals are available if you didn't bring your own.

BELOW: Boone Fork as seen from the bridge accessible from the Tanawha Trail bridge accessed at MP 300.

FOLLOWING SPREAD: Fall color is even more intense in misty, foggy conditions on Rough Ridge.

300 Boone Fork (3,905) 🚶

OK – as overlooks go it doesn't "look over" much. It is however, a major access point for hiking the flanks of Grandfather Mountain and the Tanawha Trail (which parallels the Parkway for 13 miles). If you are not a hiker, the short walk to the hiker's bridge over the Boone Fork is a short quarter-mile jaunt that requires no special gear. The reward is the walk itself through cool dense forest to an elevated view of the Boone Fork itself. Don't confuse this stretch with the Boone Fork

Trail mentioned recently at Price Lake – same creek, different section. For details of these hikes, see the sidebar, page 92.

302.8 Rough Ridge (4,293) 🚶

This overlook itself doesn't seem to show much, which is to say, its charms are hidden from casual view. This is, however, the **ONE HIKE YOU MUST DO**, even if you are not the hiking sort. To the right of the parking area, climb the stone steps to the Tanawha Trail intersection and turn left. Cross the footbridge and climb steadily for a few minutes to a blueberry- and laurel-lined tunnel. The trail is briefly steep, but take your time and you will be fine. The terrain soon opens up to expansive views and large rocky outcrops. An extensive boardwalk takes you safely through this fragile, rocky, heath ecosystem. The views are unparalleled, and in late May and early June the Catawba rhododendron and mountain laurel blooms are exquisite. The rare and graceful turkey beard may bloom at the same time as well. In early October, the color display here is way beyond George

On a stormy fogged-in day at the peak of fall color, Rough Ridge is a magical place. Evergreens fade like the mast of some phantom ship, only to reappear when the clouds shift. Colors become super saturated and vibrant. Put on your wet-weather gear for an unforgettable experience.

Eastman's wildest dreams, with scarlet blueberry bushes offsetting the incandescent red, orange and yellow shades of maples and mountain ash. Bring sunglasses, even in the fog. The color is that intense. Really.

Beyond the wooden platforms, the trail grows steeper, and becomes more of a serious hike as it climbs the ridge above. More dynamic scenes await, but you have seen some of the best by now, and if you are not a serious hiker, you can retrace your steps. The Tanawha Trail continues to Wilson Creek, and beyond past Linn Cove Visitor Center to its terminus at Beacon Heights. Beautiful in all conditions, this mountainside takes on a special magic in fog, when the weather is otherwise frightful. Be prepared for

gusty breezes too, they didn't call it "rough" for nothing. Allow at least 45 minutes to walk to the boardwalk, hang out and return, 2 hours to the top of the ridge and back.

304 Linn Cove 🚶 Viaduct (4,412)

The Yonahlossee overlook, just north of the Viaduct at MP 303.9, is the easier of two access points to see the classic view. Park here and follow the shoulder on the safe side of the guardrail. As you approach the viaduct itself, look for a steep scramble up the side of the hill. Climb about 30 steep feet up to a rocky shelf with views of the sinuous graceful viaduct below. Look for the Tanawha Trail immediately beyond. This viewpoint is also accessible from the visitor center, with a bit more hiking involved. The curve in the road south of the parking area is a popular site for sunrise photography. White blooming sarvis trees grow nearby, and goldenrod line the road in late summer and early fall. Allow 20 minutes for a peek, longer to photograph.

Photo Notes

Photographers wishing to make images of the viaduct will find early to mid-morning light the most pleasing. The flanks of Grandfather are prone to gusty winds, but this cove is relatively sheltered, even when the ground is shaking just around the bend at the parking area.

The viaduct has infinite moods depending on time of day and weather conditions. It receives sidelight from the morning sun (better photos) and is in shadow in the afternoon.

304.4 Linn Cove Visitor Center (4,315) ❓🥾👫

The visitor center parking area offers access to the Tanawha Trail as it courses through dense forest and huge boulders to wooded views of the partially obscured Linn Cove Viaduct. It leads to the previously mentioned viewpoint overlooking the graceful curves of this internationally acclaimed engineering achievement. The Viaduct was the centerpiece of the last section of the Parkway to be completed. Construction techniques used in Europe, not available when Parkway construction began, minimized environmental impact resulting in the structure you see today. Each section was precast and lowered into place, each building upon the last. No two of the 153 segments are alike and only one is straight. The only trees sacrificed were those immediately beneath the span.

305 Beacon Heights (4,220) 🥾

This large parking area is among the most popular with local residents and with good reason. The main action is not the view here, though Grandfather presents an impressive profile and is quite satisfying, thank you. The main event here is Beacon Heights itself, two large rocky shelves providing outstanding views in a pristine setting. Fortunately, unlike Humpback Rocks, there is a noticeable absence of spray paint. For your viewing convenience there is a morning location and an afternoon location. They are both gorgeous, but time of day favors one, then the other. This is one of the premier sunrise locations for photography on the entire Parkway, and a fair option for evening light.

The rocky domes at Beacon Heights make great locations for photography or just stopping to enjoy the views. They slope steeply towards the edge, and the lichens become slick as a cheap politician when wet after rain or heavy fog. A slip could have fatal consequences; don't get too close to the edge. It's not an abrupt cliff, which makes it less intimidating, but no less risky.

Here, morning light illuminates a blueberry bush on Beacon Heights' rocky platform. There are great views of Grandfather over your shoulder on the east side of the Heights.

From the overlook, cross the small paved road (not the Parkway) and enter the woods beyond. Turn right at the junction with the Tanawha and Mountains to the Sea Trail to ascend a moderate grade. In a few hundred yards, leave the Mountains to the Sea Trail and ascend to the left and approach the crest. Here, close to a convenient bench, the trail forks offering access to two large rocky domes. Climb steep stone steps to the left for morning vistas of Pisgah National Forest, the unheralded Globe Forest (and an old growth oak stand) and the Wilson Creek drainage. The right hand fork takes you to the west-facing dome which receives evening light. Here are views of the twin peaks of Hawksbill and Table Rock in distant Linville Wilderness, and Mount Mitchell. Allow at least 30 minutes for a quick look, hours for an in-depth visit.

exit
305

Grandfather Mountain

U.S. 221 takes you one mile south to the entrance to this outstanding, privately owned, preserve. Personally, I am not a fan of tourist traps; I like my *nature*, well,

Mountain Ash berries frame Grandfather's twin peaks in early fall.

natural, and free from as much human interference as possible. So you should take what I have to tell you with that in mind. Grandfather is much more than a tourist attraction, certainly not a trap; it is truly a preserve in the broadest sense of the word.

Here the business world melded with the world of nature and produced a whole greater than the sum of its parts. The paradigm shift together with the surging environmental awareness that swept the nation in the 1960s and 70s infected Hugh Morton as it did so many others. Morton, the owner and driving force behind Grandfather Mountain, was an accomplished nature photographer in his own right, and that love of nature and this mountain transformed the organization, resulting in the place you can visit today. This isn't an amusement park. It's all about nature, presented in the highest quality fashion.

Grandfather is the only privately held property to pass the rigorous certification requirements to be designated as an International Biosphere Preserve by UNESCO, a branch of the United Nations. A yearly recertification process assures that the designation is not just advertising fluff. Additionally, land not essential to the core revenue-generating operations is held in trust by the Nature Conservancy with restrictive covenants regarding use and development, protecting over 3000 acres in all. The Conservancy assists in managing the biological resources of the tract, and Grandfather additionally employs its own naturalist team.

So what's the big deal? Grandfather Mountain, like several similar high peaks is home to a different ecosystem, a holdover from the retreat of the last glaciers. The mountain is home to 16 distinct natural communities, with 70 rare or endangered species, 29 that are globally imperiled. You would have to journey far to the north to find these high alpine micro-climes. The 2.7-mile Profile Trail, for instance, takes you through seven distinct natural communities.

Grandfather's stunning scenery is accessible to people of all ages and fitness lev-

Photo Notes

Your images will be more attractive in soft, cloudy or misty conditions, unless you have warm low directional light. The harsh shadows cast by the bright overhead sun seriously detract from the quality of most wildlife photos. If you have time, and are after higher quality images, consider coming back to the wildlife habitat when the sun is lower, if you are visiting on a blue-sky day.

LEFT: The usual list of suspects.

RIGHT: A late spring display of fern, thyme leaved bluets, and rhododendron petals.

els, but not everyone should tackle the backcountry. There are short walks, long rugged hikes, a picnic area, wildlife habitat area and lots of gorgeous scenery.

Children of all ages enjoy the wildlife habitat, even octogenarian type children; it's not your ordinary zoo. To begin with, the resident critters can't or shouldn't be released into the wild. The bald eagles were severely injured by hunters in western states, and placed here by the U.S. Fish and Wildlife Agency, who regulate all captive bald eagles. Mildred the Bear was Grandfather Mountain's first mascot, brought from the Atlanta Zoo's release program to reintroduce black bears on the mountain, but she failed in the wild. She soon became famous herself in a specially designed habitat and became a focal point for many visitor's mountain experience. Previously, bears born in the preserve would be released in the wild after being prepped for the experience, but released bears don't always do well. With the potential for deaths due to poaching, legal hunting, and traffic related injuries,

a birth control program is in place. Any cubs you see are non-releasable animals brought here from a rehab center. The two cougars were born in captivity in educational facilities, and are not able to be released into the wild. Deer, river otters and a golden eagle also call the mountain home, and if not wild, their hangout is the closest thing to it. They are usually fairly cooperative for the camera as well; in fact, the wildlife images in this book were all created in about a 45 minute time frame. Sections of the habitat are wheelchair accessible with some assistance. Adjacent to the wildlife habitat is the museum with a minerals display, photo gallery, reception area, and café. Many photographs deck the walls in the gallery area. that were taken by students at the annual photo workshops The minerals gallery is a must for rock hounds. An enormous amethyst is nearly three feet across.

THE MILE HIGH SWINGING BRIDGE

This 220-foot suspension bridge spans an 80-foot-wide cleft to provide access to Linville Peak. Built in 1952 and refurbished in 1999, it was a key attraction in the early days of developing Grandfather as a tourist destination. It provides access to nearby Linville Peak with additional views; there is an adjacent visitor center where you can warm up or dry off during foul weather. The parking area for the bridge is the higher of the jumping-off points for the rugged backcountry as well.

THE INCREDIBLE GRANDFATHER BACKCOUNTRY

Wowsers! This incredibly rugged and beautiful alpine environment is calling YOU! The five-mile round-trip hike to Calloway Peak will take you five hours or more depending on your fitness level and number of stops. Happily, for the less adventurous, the trip can be broken up into several shorter, more bite-sized pieces; MacRae Peak is less than a mile out (still a two-hour round trip). Along the way you will pass through an alpine wonderland, traverse ladders up rock faces normally reserved for technical climbers, and have a hike like no other in the area. Indeed, several well-traveled hikers have compared the rock faces to the granite wonderland at Yosemite. Several shorter hikes offer more options.

The Nuwati, Cragway and Daniel Boone Scout Trails (trailhead at Boone Fork Overlook, MP 300) quickly cross Grandfather Mountain boundaries. You need to get the inexpensive, hiking-only, permit at the entrance gate or at one of several area outlets to hike these trails. Park entrance fees **include** hiking for the day, and a season pass covers it all for one year. There are several overnight backcountry campsites available. "Leave-no-trace" practices are in effect. Call 828-737-0833 for details, and the closest location where you can pick up a permit; the fees support trail maintenance.

Modern day "chutes and ladders" will take you further than that childhood board game. The ladders are the only safe way for mere mortals to navigate the rocky headwalls of the Grandfather backcountry.

You will often be in or above the clouds; sometimes the "fog" can be quite thick. The trails is well marked, and when in doubt or on very rocky terrain, blue blazes and arrows point the way. Stormy weather can be hazardous, both from slips on wet rocks as well as electrical events. High winds sometimes close the access road, as do snow and ice.

The luxuriant blueberry patches offer gastronomic followed by visual delights in late summer and fall. Sand myrtle, mountain laurel, and Catawba rhododendron are among the late spring and early summer blooms.

PRECEDING PAGES AND LEFT:

The rugged Grandfather Trail provides access to some of the wildest and most remote country in the eastern U.S.

HIKING TIPS

1. Supportive boots are highly recommended. It has been done in tennis shoes, but you might pay for it later. Twisted ankles not withstanding, some stress injuries take months to heal (plantar fasciitis, Achilles tendonitis), and it might take a few days to realize you have even been hurt.

2. A hiking staff (two are even better than one) add a lot of stability and balance on the downhill, reducing falls and ankle injuries. Europeans routinely use a pair; looks a little goofy at first, but they are worth it. You can even get a little boost on the uphill.

3. Carry water and snacks. You will probably need both. Dehydration sneaks up on you when climbing these steep trails. Carry some form of water purification device on longer hikes. You might otherwise take home an unwanted and expensive souvenir from drinking unpurified water.

4. Carry appropriate storm gear. Rain is common, as is wind, and at the high peaks (nearly 6,000 feet high) conditions can be drastically different than at the trailhead, and change suddenly. The wind chill factor can become dangerously low and induce hypothermia, even in summer. Descend quickly in the event of electrical storms.

PARKWAY-ACCESSIBLE GRANDFATHER TRAILS

These are detailed in various hiking guides, and on the Grandfather Mountain map that you receive when you pick up your permit. Please note you are on private property once you leave the Tanawha Trail. Your user fees directly maintain these fine trails. These Parkway-accessible trails originate at Boone Fork Overlook, MP 300. You can mix and match these trails according to time available, weather and your fitness. Take a map and compass. The Grandfather trail map is sufficient for basic navigation. That map's scale makes the trails appear more mellow than they are. Many have a 1,000 foot-per-mile grade!

The Nuwati (Cherokee, loosely translated, "medicine, good medicine of life") Trail begins after a 0.4-mile walk to the west on the Tanawha (Cherokee, "fabulous hawk") Trail. Take the right hand branch 1.2 miles to Boone Fork bowl, and the immense Storyteller Rock. This trail is relatively gentle, but rather rocky, and rates moderate towards the end. Four backcountry campsites offer overnight options, and there is water along the way (purify please).

A little over half a mile up the Nuwati brings you to the junction with the Cragway Trail that connects it to the Daniel Boone. Periodic rock outcroppings adorn the trail, offering excellent views, and a chance to catch your breath on this steep pitch that gains over 800 feet in one short mile. Take your time, and if you aren't heavily laden with photo or overnight gear, you will be just fine. At this (possibly welcome) junction, you can head downhill to complete a four-mile loop, or if you first went on to the end of the Nuwati, an almost six-mile loop. A short trek further up hill gets you to a campsite and a fairly reliable spring (look for the spring trail on the other side of the campsite).

The Daniel Boone Scout Trail continues up the ridge line to Calloway Peak and the intersection with the high Grandfather Trail. It then leads to the main visitor center and swinging bridge, reaching it in another steep (almost 1,000 vertical feet) mile. Along the way you will pass more views and additional campsites. To bypass the Nuwati and ascend a bit more gradually, hike westward about another quarter mile to the intersection with the Scout Trail and ascend more directly to the summit. As you near, be prepared for some scrambling and a ladder. Those with a fear of heights will need to consider this last pitch carefully; it's safe, but a bit exposed, and might induce a sense of vertigo in one so inclined.

The Tanawha Trail is by now familiar sounding, and easily hiked. This public (no access fee) trail connects Beacon Heights with Price Park campground and picnic area, and its 13.5-mile length closely parallels the Parkway. Indeed, traffic noises are often completely muffled by the dense surrounding woods, the road seldom seen. Many visitors hike only short portions of the trail, such as at Rough Ridge, discussed previously. If you wish to tackle the entire length, arrange a shuttle or stash a bike at one end. You can get a free map at the Linn Cove Visitor Center.

7

Linville Falls

Crabtree falls

MP 315 - 340

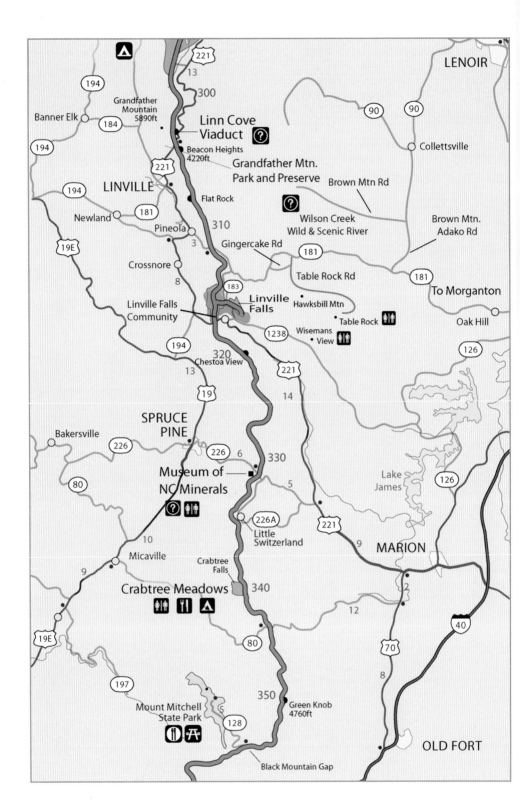

Table Rock graces the skyline with the sun shining through the poplars near MP 331

MP	POINT OF INTEREST	FEATURES	
Exit 312	Hawksbill Mountain & Table Rock , south on NC 181	Hike to scenic summits, access to Linville Gorge Wilderness	
316.5	Linville Falls	Scenic waterfall, hiking	
Exit 317.4	Wisemans View – take U.S. 221, south to Linville Falls Community (see text)	Scenic overlook, multiple hiking options in Linville Gorge Wilderness	
320.8	Chestoa View	Scenic overlook, spring wildflowers	
331	Museum of N.C. Minerals	Visitor center, museum	
339	Crabtree Falls	Hike to scenic waterfall, camping	
MP	**LODGING, DINING & GAS**	**MP**	**CAMPING**
312	NC 181 — north to Pineola and Newland — gas only, (S) 2 miles	316.5	Linville Falls CG - BRP facility
317.4	U.S. 221 — south to Linville Falls Community	339	Crabtree Falls CG - BRP facility
331	NC 226 — west to Spruce Pine	**MP**	**HOSPITAL**
334	Little Switzerland	312	NC 181 — 30 miles (S) Morganton **Grace Hospital** 828-580-5000
MP	**RESTAURANT ONLY**	331	NC 226 — 5 miles west **Spruce Pine Community Hospital** 828-765-4201
339	Crabtree Meadows (seasonal)		

OVERVIEW

Well, you'll hardly have time to get settled in your seat before you get to the next major scenic area on the Parkway at MP 316.5. The Linville Falls area was a resort destination long before the Parkway came into being, drawing visitors to see the fabulous falls, clear waters, deep rugged gorge and stands of virgin timber. Modern-day visitors can enjoy a casual visit, via a 1.4-mile long spur road off the Parkway and a one-mile gentle round-trip hike to see the Falls, or spend days hiking the steep wilderness trails in the 12,000-acre Linville Gorge Wilderness. Shorter hikes in the wilderness area allow day tripping and are practical options for anyone fit for hiking. The trails are not wheelchair accessible, though the visitor center is. Details of the various options around Linville Falls and adjacent wilderness follow shortly.

The Linville River begins as a trickle on the flanks of Grandfather Mountain, and as it gathers steam, cuts a steep rocky gorge, dropping almost 2000 vertical feet in 12 miles from the Falls itself to Lake James in the Piedmont below. Named "Eeseeoh, River of Many Cliffs", by the Cherokee, it was re-named in honor of William Linville, an early explorer who was killed by a raiding party of northern Indians in 1766. John D. Rockefeller purchased land surrounding the falls and subsequently donated the parcel to the National Park Service in 1952. The 440-acre Falls tract is adjacent to the larger 12,000-acre Linville Gorge Wilderness, which was designated in the first round of selection when the original Wilderness Act was signed into law in 1964.

LEFT: Linville Falls has many moods and a thorough exploration of this special place requires more than one visit. Sunny days aren't the best for photography as a general rule, but all rules were meant to be broken and late afternoon light can be pleasing as from Erwins view.

RIGHT: Carolina rhododendrons add a special accent in early May before the more colorful and well known Catawba rhododendron open up. This variety has smaller paler flowers, and smaller leaves. They are plentiful atop Hawksbill as well.

The roads in and around Linville Falls get a little tricky; a detailed road map is helpful. As you near Linville Falls you will pass NC 181 heading south at MP 312. You soon reach NC 183, which parallels the Parkway to the west passing an alternate entry to the Falls area and on to the community of Linville Falls. NC 181 takes you south to Hawksbill Mountain and Table Rock, both key features of the Linville Gorge Wilderness Area.

NC 181 is also your connection to the Wilson Creek Wild and Scenic River. Follow it south about nine miles to the now conjoined Adako-Brown Mountain Beach Road (NC 90). Turn left (east) and continue for about four miles to SR 1328 Brown Mountain Beach Road (Adako Road continues to the east). Turn left (north) and pass a commercial campground with seasonal store and within about two miles you will be driving along the banks of this exquisite mountain stream. This is a favorite of whitewater boaters who drive many hours for a chance to paddle its big drops and intricate rapids. To you, big rapids means scenery. Extensive public lands, a network of Forest Service roads, multiple trails and waterfalls and fishing opportunities wait for the off-Parkway explorer. There is a backdoor entry from the Parkway at MP 311.1 on an unsigned Forest Road. A map, a sense of adventure, a full gas tank and time to kill are all essential; it's easy to get lost going in to Wilson Creek by the back door.

The small resort community of Linville Falls offers lodging, dining and gas — a perfect stopover for lunch or for the evening. When the Parkway itself is closed due to snow and ice, a lower trailhead to the falls is accessible from NC 183 going east out of town. U.S. 221 south leads to I-40 near Marion, North Carolina, offering easy access from the south and east

The Linville Gorge Trail descends steeply to the waters edge in about three fourths of a mile. From there make your way along the bank upstream to views of the Falls. The current can be quite strong here, even in low water. Higher flows are deceptively dangerous.

RIGHT: The Bynum Bluff trail drops steeply into the gorge from the road leading to Wisemans View (SR 1238). This is one of seven trails to descend from the west side to the river corridor that provides a streamside experience, fishing and relative solitude. The Linville Gorge Trail follows the west bank for over 11 miles before leaving the gorge. This trail bears the same name but is not contiguous with the Gorge Trail that descends to the plunge basin below the falls.

for folks who didn't have time for a top-to-bottom Parkway drive. Access from the north side of the Parkway is probably easiest via U.S. 19E from Elizabethton, Tennessee to NC 194 to NC 181 at Newland, to U.S. 221 and entry at Grandfather and Beacon Heights at MP 305.

Continuing south, you will soon find Chestoa View overlook at MP 320.8. The stonework itself is quite scenic, as is the view, though of late it is a bit grown over. The expansive view is impressive, and there is a short trail that follows the rim, offering a leg-stretching option for anyone who passed up the falls and wants a little exercise. In late April and early May, acres of trillium and may apple cover the forest floor nearby, creating one of the Parkway's premier wildflower shows. You will soon reach a set

of descending radius spiral turns. These are tricky due to the increasing tightness of the turn; extra caution advised. The Parkway rambles on past the Orchard at Alta Pass, MP 328.3, where you can enjoy local crafts, products, history and music. On September 29th, re-enactors celebrate the passage of the Overmountain Men, who passed through here to the battle of King's Mountain, a decisive battle of the American Revolution. Traditional musicians perform here on weekends during the operating season.

The Museum of North Carolina Minerals is adjacent to the Parkway at Gillespie Gap MP, 331. The museum hosts a visitor center and mining exhibits. A re-enactment is also held here in mid-September. Off-Parkway services are available close by in Spruce Pine.

Three miles further brings you to the resort community of Little Switzerland, deeply steeped in Parkway history.

Crabtree Falls is the main natural feature of Crabtree Meadows Recreation Area at MP 339. It also features a campground, seasonal restaurant with gift shop and picnic area. Through travelers, and those familiar with the Parkway, know this is one of two waterfalls on or near the Parkway bearing the same name. The Virginia waterfall is near, but not on the Parkway itself. This fall drops in a single tier, reached on a 2.5-mile loop trail of moderate difficulty.

While most of us tend to lump all these mountains loosely into the "Blue Ridge" you southbound travelers are soon going to depart the Blue Ridge Mountains proper, and will pass a succession of smaller sub-ranges—the Blacks, Craggies, Pisgah Ledge, Balsams and Plott Balsams—as you approach the Great Smokies, 130 miles distant.

316.5 Linville Falls (3,160)

The spur road leading to the visitor center and trailhead passes by the campground and a riverside overlook before reaching the parking area. The size of this parking area will give you some idea of the falls' popularity, but don't be dissuaded from parking and putting on your walking shoes. The overlooks are rarely overcrowded, given several trail options and inevitable crowd dispersal. The visitor center is staffed with friendly informative folks who can update you on trail conditions and what's blooming, provide you with a map and set you on your way. Large signs detail the hiking options and trail system and feature photos of the falls to give you some visual orientation. Visit times vary.

The Linville Falls Trail is *THE* avenue for viewing the falls. Cross Linville River on the footbridge behind the visitor center climb the gentle path gradually to three spur trails that lead to views of the falls. The first spur, at 0.5 miles, leads to views of the upper falls; the Chimney View (highly recommended) spur departs at 0.6 miles, and continues on to Erwins View at about 0.8 miles. Each viewpoint provides a different perspective: Upper Falls provides views of the slot through which the river plunges, as well as a smaller upstream cascade, but not views

At Wisemans View, left, dramatic views of Table Rock and Hawksbill Mountain fill the skyline and you have downstream views of the gorge below. Some call this "the Grand Canyon of the East." Hyperbole notwithstanding, it's an impressive sight.

LEFT: Crimson sumac leaves frame Table Rock at Wisemans View.

RIGHT: The deciduous rock layers atop Hawksbill Mountain frame the view looking across to the western escarpment of the gorge.

of the main drop. Chimney View is the classic, most-oft-photographed vantage point, and Erwins View offers a different perspective as well as views downstream. If your time or energy is limited, put your effort into Chimney View; it's not much further and not much more work.

You will pass a side trail at 0.4 miles to an "overflow" parking area. You can reach that trailhead following NC 183 one mile from the junction with U.S. 221 in the community of Linville Falls. You will see a prominent sign for the wilderness area and falls where it joins SR 1238 that leads to Wisemans View. If you are in the community of Linville Falls, or if the Parkway is closed, this trailhead provides another access point for the falls.

Three trails offer hiking options on the East side of the river. These start behind the visitor center and head briefly up-hill through rhododendron tunnels before leveling off and descending to the Plunge Basin View and the gorge floor. Leaving the trailhead, Duggers Creek Trail branches off and loops back to the parking area's far side, crossing (what else) Duggers Creek with views of a small cascade. At about a quarter mile, the Plunge Basin Trail descends to a stone-walled overlook providing a side profile view of the falls. This view is not as popular with photographers, but the view is impressive. Bypassing this spur, continue on the Linville Gorge Trail and descend steeply through more rhododendron tunnels to the river's bank in about three-fourths mile. Scramble upstream at water's edge to views of the falls below the base of the plunge pool. There aren't any connectors here, so it's really a down-and-back jaunt. The trail sees relatively light use so it's a good way to escape the crowds if there are lots of tour buses in the parking area.

WISEMANS VIEW

Exit MP 317.4 to U.S. 221 south to Linville Falls community. Turn left at the NC 183 Junction. One mile from 221, look for the sign, leave the pavement and follow SR 1238. You will find the seasonal visitor center four-tenths of a mile on your right. This is under Forest Service management, a distinction of little import to the average visitor, but *THEY* have the wilderness information you need if you plan to hike any of the trails into the gorge. Stop in for a chat and current information, as well as maps.

Follow SR 1238 for four miles to the parking area for Wisemans View. A gentle quarter-mile trail leads to spectacular views of Hawksbill and Table Rock across the way, and views of Linville Gorge, 1,500 feet below.

Along the road, you will have passed several trailheads that offer access to the gorge below. They are linked near the river by the Linville Gorge Trail, which provides loop hike options galore. A shuttle vehicle is helpful, but not essential. Allow at least 1 hour to see Wisemans view and return to Linville Falls.

HAWKSBILL MOUNTAIN

A short steep hike leads to one of the Southeast's premier wilderness destinations. It combines breathtaking scenery with fantastic rock shapes, and is a short enough hike that the steep grade will not be overly tiring. It is THE place to be for those wanting to escape the crowds in the Linville Falls area, and is a photographer's wonderland. No special gear is required, you don't need 4WD or anything exotic, but a map is helpful.

Exit the Blue Ridge Parkway on NC 181 heading south at MP 312. In 4.6 miles

Hawksbill summit is an inspiring place. You can feel the energy that wild places impart like few other locations in the southeast. This is a rather arid microclime, with Table Mountain Pines and a heath community eking out a living. Exposed to desiccating winds and growing in shallow, nutrient-poor soils, it's a wonder anything thrives here at all, but this unique plant community finds its niche. In early May the Carolina rhododendron, turkey beard and sand myrtle grace the broad plateau that is Hawksbill summit.

LEFT: A small colony of Carolina rhododendron clings to the cliffside overlooking the gorge below.

RIGHT: A luxuriant growth of sand myrtle, with Grandfather and Roan Mountain on the distant skyline. Though small in this image, to the left on the skyline, the large condominium complex at Sugar Top is easily (all too easily) visible, from over 25 miles away. This structure sparked such a controversy that North Carolina passed a law regulating ridgetop construction.

turn right at the Forest Service placard signed for Table Rock. You will be on Gingercake Road, which soon forks and loops back to NC 181 behind you. Take the left fork at this intersection onto Table Rock Road, passing through the vacation home development of Gingercake Acres, and leave the pavement about a mile after turning off NC 181. Follow the usually well-graded road along a contour, past fern groves and past the Sitting Bear trailhead to the trailhead for Hawksbill 3.6 miles after leaving highway 181. Park here and find the trail across from the parking area. The trail climbs steeply for almost a half mile before leveling out to a gentler grade. Be alert for a trail going uphill to your left. If you missed this trail intersection, which many do, you will reach a post that has

lost its sign; turn back and retrace your steps and the proper route will become evident. The trail to the top climbs steeply again for a little less than a half mile to the broad summit's rocky shelf.

The summit is breathtaking, a power point where you can feel the energy of the wild place you are visiting. This is a fragile place as well. There is no water other than that provided by rain, and fire scars from careless campers are all too evident. Wildfire is an ever-present threat, and while flame is essential to germinate seeds of some of the resident flora, please don't take that to mean a fire up here is OK.

As you ascend to the summit you will be at an intersection of social trails and

meanders. Wander to the south and to the north at this juncture for equally interesting views and rock formations. To the south, view the distinctive summit of Table Rock; to the west, the broad summit of Linville Mountain; and to the northeast, Grandfather, Roan Mountain, and the unfortunate square silhouette of Sugar Top condominium complex. This artificial addition to the skyline prompted passage of the North Carolina Ridge Law which prohibits construction of any building that exceeds 40 feet in height on ridge-lines above 3,000 feet elevation (communication towers are sadly exempt).

In early May, enjoy the blooms of the uncommon Carolina rhododendron known locally as periwinkle. This little known variety of rhododendron varies from pale pink to an intense hue that ri-

val the magenta blooms of the Catawba rhododendron. It blooms earlier than the Catawba variety; when its blossoms are falling, the Catawba are entering prime condition. Be alert for peregrine falcon sightings, they have been repopulating the gorge.

You can catch sunset from Hawksbill summit and hike back down to your car before it's pitch black but the woods can be quite dark. Take a flashlight or head lamp. The downhill journey is steep, and can get slick; trekking poles are useful here. The extra balance point goes a long way to reducing falls and ankle sprains.

TABLE ROCK

Continue on past the Hawksbill trailhead another six miles to Table Rock. The last mile and a half are again paved,

The views must have been wide open when the overlook was first constructed, but the forest is reclaiming her own. Opposite the parking area and in the surrounding mile you will find dense extensive growth of may apple and *trillium grandiflora*, the large white flowering trillium. Look for may apple blooms underneath the broad leaf canopy. Peak bloom is usually in late April and early May.

339 Crabtree Falls (3,500)

Crabtree Meadows provides a hub of activity and overnight camping for the Parkway visitor between Linville Falls and the high country of Mount Mitchell and Craggy Gardens to the south. The campground, store and restaurant allow a casual overnight for those so equipped, and the picnic area provides a lunch stop for passers by. Crabtree Falls is the key feature, and is one of the finest waterfalls in the state, never mind along the Parkway. You waterfall lovers can easily make this moderate hike in the same afternoon that you visit Linville Falls if you don't make the climb to Hawksbill Mountain.

and you will see why. This last segment is a stress test for your transmission and brakes; did I say STEEP? At the summit you will find a picnic area, rest rooms and hiking trails. This area is a favorite for rock climbers. Trail options include the summit trail, the Mountains-to-Sea Trail again, and the Little Table Rock Trail that connects to Spence Ridge and the gorge below. The summit trail is about 0.75 miles in length and leads to craggy views and the chance to see rock climbers in action.

320.8 Chestoa View (4,090)

This viewpoint itself takes only a few minutes to enjoy, and superb wildflower displays are in easy walking distance in season. Park and descend the stone steps to a small stone balcony overlooking the valley and ridges below. A short leg-stretcher trail follows the rim of the escarpment for about a half-mile loop.

The trailhead and falls parking area are immediately behind the campground entry station. The well-maintained loop trail drops steadily at first, then steeply down a series of wooden stairs before reaching the falls in a little less than a mile. Cross the bridge below the falls to the far side for the best views. Continue on the loop to return to your car for a total of 2.5 miles, or retrace your steps for a slightly shorter hike. Allow at least an hour round trip plus time at the falls.

LEFT: Sunrise at Chestoa View Overlook. **RIGHT:** Crabtree Falls in spring colors. **BELOW:** Sunbeams break through the fog near Gillespie Gap.

 ## PHOTO NOTES

Fog settles in the gaps before dawn and rises with the warming sun. If you are chasing fog or light beams, drive down to an elevation that is just below the fog line for breaking light beams, or lower for more moody scenes.

You can predict fog rather easily. Check the weather forecast for the dew point and the lowest early morning temperatures. If they are within 2 or 3 degrees of each other there will be fog in the valleys, denser if it rained the night before, or warmed up after a cool spell.

109

MORE PHOTO NOTES

The falls face east. They will be in shade in mid-to-late afternoon, giving soft but bluish light if you need to photograph on a sunny day. Small rainbows will form in the mist when the sun is shining over your shoulder in the morning hours. On a cloudy days you can enjoy the soft light at your leisure. Fall color peaks here a little sooner than you might think based on what's happening in the surrounding areas, often by mid-October.

Add variety to your images by trying different angles and compositions. Look for both vertical and horizontal variations, and try including foreground elements that add impact and a sense of season and place. A slower shutter speed adds a silky texture to the water; a tripod is helpful. Be watchful for water droplets landing on your lens when photographing in the rain or around waterfalls. You can end up with unexpected blobs in your final image as you can see below.

DEATH *in the* FOREST

The majestic Eastern and Carolina hemlocks in Linville Gorge have seen more history than most of have forgotten from our school days, likely more than most of us ever learned. Some were little more than seedlings when our country was young, others old when the Constitution was signed. They were saved from the axe and saw by their remote location and by nature-loving landowners before being acquired by John D. Rockefeller and donated to the Blue Ridge Parkway in the 1950s. Not enough will be saved again.

A miniscule insect, the Hemlock Woolly Adelgid, is bringing down towering forest giants in mind-numbing numbers. The pest has been with us for many decades, slowly working its way down the southern Appalachian chain, and moving much more quickly than anyone predicted. western hemlocks showed natural resistance and no one paid any mind when the pest was first noticed over 80 years ago. Eastern hemlocks and the less common Carolina hemlock had no natural resistance, but the initial infestation showed up in landscaped settings where the trees could be sprayed or replanted; no one paid much mind. The genie is now out of the bottle. Widespread devastation has struck our southern mountains, with die-off seen from Shenandoah to the Smokies, in the Chattooga River corridor, in the old growth stands at Joyce Kilmer Memorial Forest, and in the Cumberlands.

National Park and Forest Service personnel watched grimly but could do little. Budgetary limitations didn't help, but there weren't many effective weapons. Research has showed that a predatory beetle, similar to our ladybug and native to the pest's Asian home could have some impact, but it takes about 10,000 beetles to clean one tree. Years of testing was needed to determine that the "cure" wasn't going to be another kudzu disaster, and along with a lack of funding, delayed deployment of the beetle into a real world test drive. To date, limited numbers have been released; cost and availability are ongoing obstacles.

Spraying works, but is impractical on a towering forest giant in a remote location. Each needle has to be treated, and it has to be done yearly. Injecting trees with an insecticide has proven effective, but is labor intensive. Unfortunately, by the time that modality can be deployed, the forest will be on life support, if not DOA. Infected trees show dull needles that fall easily; once that process starts the tree has a three to five-year life expectancy; maybe a little more if the winters are sufficiently cold. The recent spate of warm winters hasn't helped much, and no climatological relief is in sight.

Sadly, scenes such as the east wall of Linville Gorge (image right) that shocked and saddened me in the fall of 2006 are becoming widespread. The visual and aesthetic impact is immediate, but the hemlock plays a complex role wherever it is either

dominant or prominent; the ripple effect on the forest ecosystem is yet unmea-sured. The chestnut blight crippled the southern hardwood forest, but oaks took up the slack and filled the vacant niche. No such substitute exists for the hemlock. In-creased erosion and the warming of trout streams heretofore shaded and sheltered by these forest leviathans is inevitable. How far this will reach, no one yet knows.

FRIENDS of the Blue Ridge Parkway has been active in combating this disaster-in- the-making. To find out more and how you can help, contact **FRIENDS** at www. BlueRidgeFriends.org or call 800-228-7275 toll free. Join now!

8

MT. MITCHELL

CRAGGY GARDENS

MOUNT MITCHELL

GLASSMINE FALLS

CRAGGY PINNACLE

CRAGGY GARDENS

MP 350 - 370

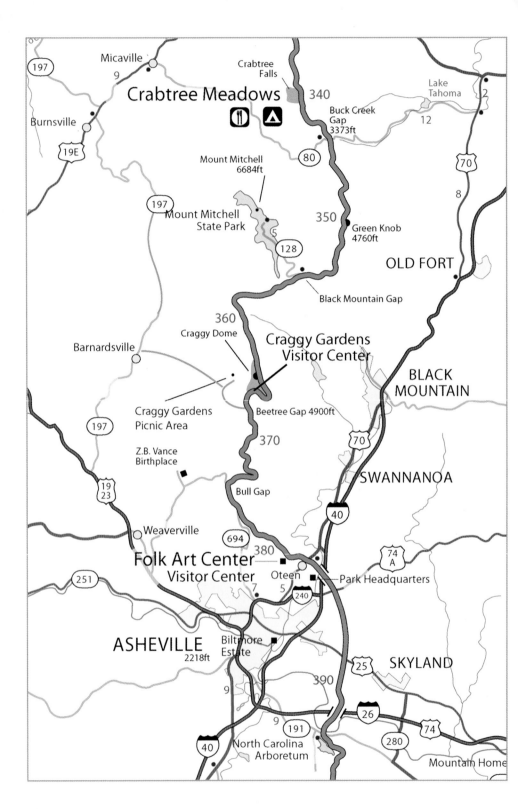

Above: Autumn tinged beech leaves glow near View Graybeard Overlook, MP 363.4.
Preceding spread: Evening glow near Craggy Gardens.

MP	POINT OF INTEREST	FEATURES
350	Green Knob Overlook	Scenic views
355.4	Mount Mitchell State Park	Highest point in eastern U.S. — hiking trails, restaurant, campground
361.2	Glassmine Falls overlook	Scenic views
364	Craggy Pinnacle, Craggy Dome Overlook	Scenic views, hiking trail, seasonal rhodo-dendron bloom (mid-June)
364.5	Craggy Gardens Visitor Center, trail to Craggy Flats	Visitor center, hiking trails
367.6	Side road to Craggy Gardens Picnic and Recreation Area	Picnic area, rest rooms, hiking trail

MP	LODGING	MP	CAMPING
388.8	U.S. 25 — 3 miles (N) to Asheville also see previous section	355.4	Mount Mitchell State Park

MP	RESTAURANTS		HOSPITAL
355.4	Mount Mitchell State Park	388.8	**Memorial Mission Hospital** 828-213-1111 — about 4 miles North of Parkway on U.S. 25

MP	GASOLINE		
382.6	U.S. 70 — Asheville, either direction, less than 1 mile		

Namesake blue ridges stack on one another as they fade into the distance as seen from Green Knob Overlook.

OVERVIEW

This next section of your Parkway tour takes you ever upward after you leave Crabtree Meadows to the views at Green Knob Overlook, MP 350. You will have passed through the Rough Ridge tunnel and should not be confused into thinking you are at that glorious location about 50 miles farther north. You are heading for the high country, indeed to eastern America's rooftop, the Black Mountains, whose high point is Mt. Mitchell, 6,684 feet tall.

You will gain over 3,000 vertical feet should you drive to the summit parking area and make the short walk to the observation tower. Along the way, thrill to the exalted views offered up by North Carolina's finest peaks and valleys. These views were a persuasive argument to route the Parkway through the Blacks and Great Craggies instead of making a northerly swing into Tennessee.

Arriving at Black Mountain Gap at MP 355.3, you should pause for a few minutes, even if you have stopped at the other excellent viewpoints along the way. Here at this overlook you can take in the crisp mountain air and the expansive views without the blur that occurs through the automobile window. It's also time to check your watch to see if time allows the side trip to Mt. Mitchell State Park. I hope you are not in too big a hurry as it would be a shame to miss this one.

Glassmine Falls as viewed from the overlook. In dry weather you can hardly tell it's there, but, following a wet spell, it's a vigorous cascade spilling down a rock face near an old mica mine. Reputed to be 800 feet tall, the true height is likely far less.

Mount Mitchell hosts the only area restaurant, two meeting rooms, gift shop, numerous hiking trails and stunning views. Our old friend the Mountains -to-Sea Trail crosses NC 128 not far from the Parkway. Primitive campsites are available on a first come first served basis, but the nine sites are rarely all occupied.

From the Mt. Mitchell spur it is four short miles to Balsam Gap, MP 359.9. That marks the border between the Blacks and the Great Craggies, a geography factoid that you might otherwise miss. Two hiking trails cross here, the Mountains-to-Sea Trail that shadows the Parkway, and the Brush Fence Trail that descends to the north. Should you wish to take a jaunt on the Mountains-to-Sea Trail, it is across the Parkway from the parking area. Taking the Brush Fence Trail by mischance would not make you happy. What should make you happy, however, is a chance to stroll through a fabulous grove of beech trees, conveniently located across the Parkway. Follow the

Mountains-to-Sea Trail up the ridge as far as time allows; drop a vehicle here or stash a bike for a walk to Glassmine Falls Overlook and Craggy Pinnacle.

Glassmine Falls Overlook (5,197 ft.) MP 361.2, waits next. This high perch with unobstructed views looks across the valley as this ephemeral falls drops off the face of Horse Range Ridge near an abandoned namesake mica mine. It may completely dry up in very dry months, but can be quite beautiful after heavy rains. It's an easy stroll to the viewpoint, so it's worth at least a brief stop to check it out. This can be an intermediate stop on this leg of the Mountains-to-Sea Trail, whose next access area is the View Graybeard Mountain Overlook, MP 363.4.

The MST along this stretch of the Parkway is a high mountain experience more like unto Canada than the southeast. The trail wends its way through rhododendron tunnels and beech groves floored by carpets of the graceful mountain

Left: False hellebore, a.k.a. skunk cabbage, a.k.a. corn lily has been a favorite subject of photographers since the days of the glass plate. The graceful sworls, points and curves take on a sensual quality of infinite variety.

Common at such alpine elevations, they are found in few other places in the southeast. You can find them along many high country trails including the Old Mt. Mitchell trail north of the restaurant parking area, and in large colonies in the meadow below the restaurant. They are at their best soon after emerging from their winter sleep, usually late April to early May at this altitude. Bugs love 'em; the leaves get chewed up quickly as the season progresses.

Facing Page: Rhododendron grace Mt. Mitchell's landscape.

oat grass, ferns and trilliums. It is otherworldly. Park at either overlook for a brief out and back peak, or plan a shuttle or the ubiquitous bike stash for a longer jaunt.

Welcome to Craggy Gardens! Your first stop will be at the Craggy Dome Overlook, MP 364. Why is the parking area so big?? Because in mid-to late June when the Catawba rhododendron is blooming it might be full, that's why. A little less than half a mile south on the Parkway is the visitor center with additional hiking options as well as stunning views that require little more than bathroom slippers. From there, it's about three miles to the intersection for the spur road to Craggy Gardens Picnic Area. After this you can coast into Asheville in time for dinner, shopping or whatever suits your fancy.

355.4 Mt. Mitchell State Park

Here in the alpine zone is a unique opportunity to take a day trip far to the north. If you have been to Grandfather Mountain you have had a taste of this high alpine setting. This park has no entry fee unless you have special needs such as overnight camping. The park office is just inside the entrance gate. Pick up a map and get oriented to what's in bloom and other happenings. You can make a phone call from the pay phone here or at the restaurant if your cell phone doesn't have a signal.

The highest altitude restaurant in the east waits a half mile further up the road. The large picture window there affords

Created in 1915 with support from Governor Locke Craig (for whom Mt. Craig is named), the first North Carolina state park is clothed in history. The peak and the park were named in honor of Dr. Elisha Mitchell, explorer and science professor at the University of North Carolina. In 1844, Mitchell made altitude measurements with barometric pressures that were accurate within 12 feet of today's readings.

Later, controversy arose between Mitchell and Senator Thomas Clingman, a former student, as to which area peak had been measured and which was higher. Mitchell returned to the heights to repeat his measurements and support his claim, but slipped crossing above a waterfall and fell to his death. Clingman gave up his claim, and the highest peak was named in Mitchell's honor. His body was reburied at the summit a year after his death.

stunning views. Multiple hiking options will keep you busy for more time than a single day allows, and there are plenty of views for the non-hiker. The longer hikes are easily broken down into shorter sections for those with limited time.

The meadows below the restaurant look inviting but are a bit more rugged than they appear from above and the slope is steep and rocky. Of interest to photographers, expansive fields of false hellebore grow here. Their geometric leaves have fascinated photographers since before Ansel Adams picked up his first camera.

The paved road climbs to the summit parking area, museum, concessions and trail to the observation tower. As you near the summit you will also find a picnic area with the trailhead for the

Deep Gap Trail, and almost adjacent, the Balsam Nature Trail. A new summit observation deck will be finished by spring 2008.

Allow at least one hour to drive to the summit from the Parkway intersection, make a dash to the observation deck and depart. Allow time to linger and several hours to explore the various hiking trails.

ABOVE LEFT: The Old Mount Mitchell Trail offers hikers a boreal woodland experience with ferns, false hellebore, and rhododendron in late May and early June.

ABOVE RIGHT: The Deep Gap (Black Mountain Crest) Trail traverses dark brooding stands of red and Norway Spruce and the craggy rock outcroppings of Mt. Craig.

BOTTOM LEFT: The Mountains-to-Sea Trail parallels the Parkway, here below the summit of Potato Knob, accessed from NC 128, just off the Parkway.

MOUNT MITCHELL AREA HIKING TRAILS

Mount Mitchell offers several hiking options of varying intensity and length. Some trails ascend from lower elevations outside the park and are beyond the scope of this guide. This is a primer for those trails you can reach from the park itself and the access road, NC 128. Pick up a trail guide at the park office for additional detail.

If you look carefully, less than a half mile after you leave the Parkway driving towards Mt. Mitchell, you will see a small parking area on your right. There is a trail climbing into the trees across the road, the Mountains-to-Sea Trail again. A short out-and-back hike is well worth your time as you pass the southern flank of Potato Knob. This is another foray into the spruce-fir forest which breaks out into more open terrain populated with mountain ash and Catawba rhododendron. Follow the MST all the way to Asheville if you have the spunk and the time, or return to your vehicle when you think you have had enough fun.

As you enter the park itself, the Old Mitchell Trail offers a 2.2-mile hike from the park office with intermediate access at the restaurant 0.5 miles up the road. This hike can loop back on the Commissary Trail if you started at the park office. A short walk on this trail introduces you to the alpine spruce-fir ecosystem, found above 5,500 feet elevation. Take a short out and back walk for a few minutes in each direction if your time is limited. It becomes steep as you approach the summit. Allow 1½ to 2 hours for a leisurely hike.

The Deep Gap (Black Mountain Crest) Trail access is from the picnic area as you near the summit. It crosses Mt. Craig (the second highest eastern U.S. peak) and Big Tom before descending to its lower trailhead near Burnsville. Gaining nearly 4000 feet coming from the lowlands to the north, this trail is among the most rugged in the Eastern U.S.. An out-and-back option from the picnic area allows a moderate intensity 2.5-mile round trip along the crest to those two peaks. The really steep stuff is farther along the trail than this hike takes you. The initially well-groomed trail with convenient steps (thanks to volunteers) eventually gives way to a wilderness tread that lives up to its reputation and is briefly steep in places. The trail is a trek through dense stands of red spruce and immature Fraser firs with views from the summit of Mt. Craig on a clear day. Allow two hours round-trip to Big Tom, though if you are in a hurry and lightly laden, you might cut that estimate in half.

The Balsam Nature Trail trailhead is at the lower reaches of the summit parking area. In less than a mile, you can receive an in-depth education regarding this high alpine ecosystem and the problems it has endured. It is the most mellow of the park area trails. Allow 45 minutes to one hour to take your time and absorb what you see.

123 BEST OF THE BLUE RIDGE PARKWAY

GHOSTS IN THE FOREST

Serene, peaceful and unknowing, content to deal with the elements, the occasional hurricane and lightning strike, the Black Mountains rested relatively undisturbed long after the first Pilgrims arrived on these shores. Safe until the early 1900s, it was downhill from there; some might call it a death spiral.

Virgin until the turn of the century, the mountainside lost its innocence to the axe and saw, and witnessed nearly complete harvesting of its old growth spruce forests. The Fraser Fir a.k.a. "balsam" had fewer commercial uses, not being as fit for construction or the making of fine musical instruments, but its time was short in relative terms. Recognizing the wanton abuse of the forest, then-governor Locke Craig oversaw the creation of North Carolina's first state park in 1915, initially 525 acres in size. By then much had been lost, and worse was yet to come. Protected status stops the axe but offers no respite from pests and atmospheric pollutants.

The rapid industrialization of our country had significant environmental consequence, and budding globalization was soon to take additional toll. We gave the Europeans phyloxera, which nearly wiped out their grape producing vineyards in the old world. They repaid in kind with the Balsam Woolly Adelgid.

The adelgid is a tiny aphid-like insect that attacks mature trees and not only sucks the life out of them, but injects a toxin as well. For a time, seedlings would grow 8-10 feet high and succumb, immature trees apparently would not support an adelgid population. After depleting their food source (aka dead trees), the adelgid seemed to cycle out of the picture, but is no longer dormant and is now making another run at the forest. Recent regrowth is again threatened. More dead sticks seem inevitable. If you read the Linville section (pages 111-112) you know a little about the Hemlock Woolly Adelgid; same sort of story, a gift from our friends across the Pacific.

Industrial pollutants hit the forest also, in the form of acid rain (and acid fog). Enshrouded in cloud four days out of five, and receiving almost as much rainfall as the Pacific Northwest rainforests, the high peaks of the Blacks are bathed in rainfall whose acidity sometimes approaches that of vinegar. The weakened root systems left the tree less able to fend off pests and wind — they sickened and died.

Following deforestation, the faster growing, non-native Norway spruce was planted in the clear cuts. Similar to the red spruce, it is unfortunately not of our heritage and birthright, but a surrogate left by our own timber industry. Thank you so much. We should be grateful there are any trees at all.

So there you have it. Still wonder why you see all the dead trees? The stage was set years ago for the final chapter that played out in the early 1970s when the adelgid hit the southern Appalachians in full force. Where it stops, no one knows, but in many places the spruce-fir forest has become part briar patch, a shadow of its former self.

CRAGGY GARDENS

 364 **Craggy Pinnacle (5,640)**

The very large Craggy Dome Overlook offers views to the north and east, and an exquisite hiking opportunity. Everywhere around you are Catawba rhododendron bushes that flower in mid June. Its quite a sight anywhere near peak. The trail ascends gradually past wonderfully twisted beech trees that surely must have been in Tolkien's mind when he wrote of Middle Earth. Ascend beyond to the top of Craggy Pinnacle where trails meander off to the north, and hook back to the west to rocky balconies overlooking the Parkway, the visitor center, and the valleys below. When the bloom is in full swing expect company.

Allow one hour round-trip each for this and the following trail, plus time to gawk — possibly hours and hours.

364.5 **Craggy Gardens (5,497)**

The visitor center at Pinnacle Gap houses the usual Parkway reception facilities minus phone service. Your cell phone might work depending on your provider, but that's a small matter this close to Asheville. Catch the views across from the visitor center, being mind-

ful of traffic. Find the trailhead for the mellow Craggy Gardens Trail leading to Craggy Flats at the far south end of the large parking area. Ascend the mellow trail through rhododendron tunnels until you reach the large shelter. Here you may continue straight and descend somewhat steeply in places to the picnic area in less than a mile, or take a left hand spur to meander amongst the rhododendron on this open heath bald and climb to an elevated perch for additional views. This and the Craggy Pinnacle Trail are what all the fuss is about. In mid-June it's a MUST SEE.

367.6 Craggy Gardens Picnic and Rec. Area (4,900) ⛱ 🚻 🚶 ♿

Here a spur road climbs to a fine rhododendron-encircled picnic area and the lower trailhead for the Craggy Gardens Trail. The trail ascends at a mostly moderate grade to Craggy Flats, offering an alternate route that will be less crowded until you reach the Flats themselves.

As you get close to the picnic area you will notice a Forest Service road descending to your left. This is the Stoney Fork Road (FR 63), that leads off-Parkway via a "back door." This road becomes SR 2178 that intersects Dillingham Road; it turns left to Barnardsville and eventual interstate access to Asheville, N.C., and Tennessee. Turn right to Forest Road 74, the lower trailhead to Douglas Falls and the Craggy Mountains Scenic Area. Exploration of that area can take a full day just to scratch the surface. The descent from the picnic area is heavily rutted in the first mile or two— you will need high clearance for this side trip.

LEFT: It is just a vicious rumor. I do sometimes get out on sunny days, such as on the day this image was made at Craggy Flats.

ABOVE: Rhododendron blossoms litter the trail leading to Craggy Flats. **BELOW:** A luxuriant growth of mountain oat grass carpets the ground like waves in a green sea. Similar scenes wait for you on the trail up from the picnic area as well.

FOLLOWING SPREAD: Trees of Middle Earth, 150 yards up the Craggy Pinnacle Trail.

BAD WEATHER DAYS

Oh the weather outside is frightful, but the views can be so delightful!! Certainly bad weather days pose many challenges, from 10 miles-per-hour driving speeds in the fog, to hiking (or just getting out of the car) in the wind and rain. But foul weather days offer up some of the most amazing sights and mountain experiences to be had anywhere. Sure, you can't see very far in the fog, but... Colors become intensely saturated. Foggy scenes offer up mystery and romance. Stately spruce spires fade like the masts of a sailing ship into the gray mists. So, a bad weather day can be a day off, but it can also be the high point of your trip if you let it, "up yonder" in the clouds. Do drive safely !!

All four of these scenes await from within a few yards of Black Mountain Gap, at the junction of NC 128 leading to Mount Mitchell.

The magenta blooms of the Catawba rhododendron grace the high country in the first two weeks of June. Fall color **usually** peaks early, in the first or second week of October.

9

ASHEVILLE

FOLK ART CENTER

BILTMORE ESTATE

THE NORTH CAROLINA
ARBORETUM

MP 382 - 393

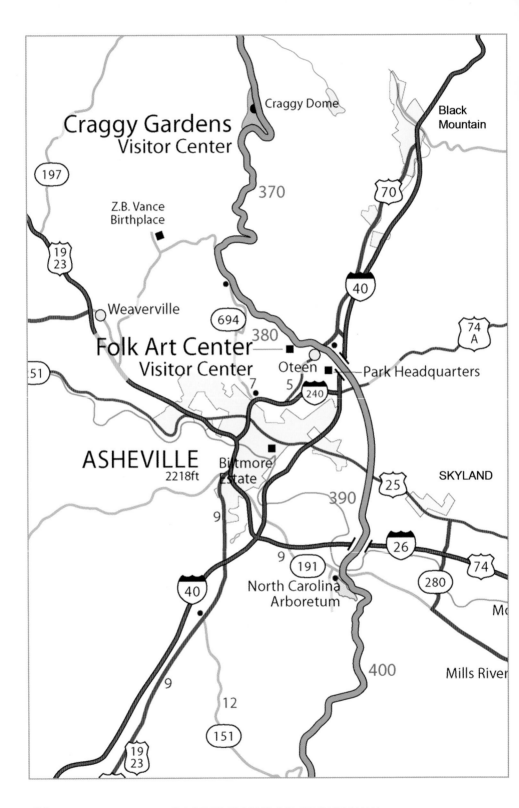

Biltmore House.
Used with permission from The Biltmore Company, Asheville, North Carolina

MP	POINT OF INTEREST	FEATURES
382	Folk Art Center	Craft and art galleries, artisans, demonstrations, exhibits, gift shop
388.8	Biltmore Estate – 3 miles north of Parkway	Biltmore House and Estate, vast grand Vanderbilt Estate, dining , lodging, multiple activities, tours
393.6	The North Carolina Arboretum entry is on the Parkway exit ramp	Extensive gardens, exhibits including the Quilt Garden, bonsai exhibits, National Native Azalea Repository, gift shop, cafe

MP	LODGING	MP	CAMPING
388.8	U.S. 25 – 3 miles north	393.6	NC 191, about 0.5 miles north to Wesley Branch Road to Lake Powhatan Rec Area (National Forest site)
393.6	NC 191 – about 2 miles north		

MP	RESTAURANTS
382.6	U.S. 70 – Less than 1 mile (W)
388.8	U.S. 25 – 1 mile both directions
393.6	NC 191 – about 2 miles north

MP	GASOLINE		HOSPITAL
382.6	U.S. 70 either direction less than 1 mile	388.8	**Memorial Mission Hospital** 828- 213-1111 about 4 miles north of Parkway on U.S. 25
384.7	U.S. 74-A – 1 mile east, 1.5 miles west		
388.8	U.S. 25 – 1.5 miles north, 0.5 miles south		
393.6	NC 191 – about 2 miles north		

Spring brings life to the English Walled Garden on Biltmore Estate.
Used with permission from The Biltmore Company, Asheville, North Carolina.

OVERVIEW

Following a tour through the lofty heights of the Blacks and the Craggies (or the high country around Mount Pisgah if coming from the south), the Parkway dips to the banks of the French Broad River and the city of Asheville. The start to finish Parkway traveler will find a warm and friendly city waiting, in which to wash off the dust from the long journey southward — or at least it used to be a dusty journey. Asheville offers a change of pace from the mountain heights, it's an upscale cosmopolitan place (the residents undoubtedly agree). Kick back and take a break from nature and incredible mountain scenery for a while; shop, dine and hang out. Asheville hosts Parkway headquarters, and several other attractions if you aren't the administrative type. Asheville is home to the Folk Art Center, Biltmore Estate and The North Carolina Arboretum — all are either on, or in close proximity to, the Parkway.

You reach the city from two major interstates, I-40 and I-26 — that's pretty much self-explanatory with a basic map. Getting into Asheville from the Parkway takes some foreknowledge, as services aren't signed on the Parkway. The lack of signage is one of the Parkway's charms, but it makes for trial and error if you don't have alternate sources of information. Driving north to south there are four exits to Asheville. The U.S. 70 crossing at MP 382.6 looks promising, but the U.S. 74-A junction a couple of miles further south at MP 384.7 is much closer to I-40. The U.S. 70 exit takes about four miles to reach I-40, while it's almost adjacent to the U.S. 74-A exit. U.S. 25, at MP 388.8 offers the most services. There you will find gas and food in the first mile both north and south of the Parkway. The justly renowned Biltmore Estate lies three miles to the north, and you will find many lodging, dining and shopping options as you near the estate. U.S. 25 crosses I-40 as you near Biltmore (exit #50 on I-40); this is also one of the best urban access points if you are entering the Parkway here from the south. At MP 393.6, exit to NC 191 and immediately find The North Carolina Arboretum. Turn left on NC 191 to reach I-26 that takes you south to Hendersonville, N.Cc and South Carolina, or north to the I-40 corridor and Asheville. This 434-acre public garden is a must see for any horticulture enthusiast and lovers of the flame azalea. The quilt garden and bonsai garden are unique and captivating.

Asheville makes a manageable base of operations for exploring the Parkway, north as far as Blowing Rock, and south as far as the Parkway terminus at MP 469 near Cherokee. There are many places of scenic interest in the surrounding mountains as well. The farther you drive, the less time you will have for other activities, so plan accordingly. Many local residents day-trip to Parkway attractions and the surrounding mountains or leave here for a weekend outing. There are multiple destinations along the Parkway in both directions giving you almost endless choices. This was resort country long ago, prized for its clean air, water, scenic beauty and cool summer temperatures. George Vanderbilt was so impressed that he chose this location for Biltmore Estate.

Intricate patterns and textures of hand blown glasswork, by Blenko Glass, online at www.blenkoglass.com. Shown by permission.

382 Folk Art Center

Much of what is now "folk art" was just "living" for our parents and grandparents in these mountains. If you needed a broom, you made one or traded for it. If your horse needed shoes, you traded for it or made your own if you had the skill and the tools. Many of these skills would have died out save for a few artisans who kept their craft and tradition alive. The Southern Highland Craft Guild which was chartered in 1930 has partnered with the National Park Service for over 50 years to help sustain and promote traditional crafts and artisanry in these southern mountains. Allanstand, the nation's first craft shop, was started by Presbyterian missionary Frances Goodrich in 1895, and continues in operation today at the Folk Art Center. When the Guild was chartered in 1930, she passed on ownership of it to provide a revenue

Need a broom? Make one, buy or barter. A traditional craft kept alive by Diana and Marlow Gates of Leicester, NC. Visit them online at www.friendswoodbrooms.com. Shown by permission.

source for continuing operations. Today you will find traditional crafts ranging from the purely functional to the purely decorative with many items joyfully having both properties about them. The display is now housed in a modern gallery, well staffed, with loads of information. One or more craftsmen (and women) are usually demonstrating their work, offering a rare chance to speak to an artist about their craft. Additional attractions are the Permanent Collection Gallery and the Robert W. Gray Library Collection, which comprises over 7,000 titles available for on site research. It is a must see stop. The Guild's web site, www.southernhighlandguild.org, provides encyclopedic information.

Sadly, some items have been photographed only to be reproduced, depriv-

ing the artist of recognition and compensation for their labors. Photography is restricted for this reason. If you wish to make photographs of any item or artisan, please inquire of the staff as to current proper procedure.

Allow a minimum of 30 minutes for a brief look up to hours and hours.

388.8 Biltmore Estate

🚻 🛏 🪑 ♿ 🍴 🚶

Biltmore Estate is Asheville's (and one of the nation's) crown jewels, a great gift to all of us from the Vanderbilt family. An entire book could be written about the estate, its history and the various attractions therein. A tour of Biltmore House is the centerpiece attraction and is a must see, particularly when Christmas approaches, as the decorations are unequaled. Time to see Biltmore

The Banquet Hall, Biltmore House.
Used with permission from The Biltmore Company, Asheville, North Carolina

House varies depending on the day of the week, time of day, season and number of visitors, as the walkway is often single file. Allow adequate time to enjoy the experience, this is not something you should rush through. The gardens are much more relaxed in that you can stroll at your whim and leisure without being dependent on crowd movements. There are float trips on the French Broad River, hiking trails, equestrian activities, bicycling, off road driving courses by the Land Rover Driving School, fly fishing courses, Segway™ tours, picnicking at your own pace and fine dining and lodging on the estate grounds. The list of activities is almost endless and of the highest caliber.

Admission and hours of operation vary seasonally. Allow at least a half day to see Biltmore House, have a brief tour of the gardens and drive through the estate. On peak visitation days a timed entry program is in effect whereby you will be given a set time to enter Biltmore House. This effectively spreads out visitation into a more manageable flow and enhances your experience. You can then tour other portions of the estate, knowing you have a set time to enter Biltmore House. Visit the web site to plan your visit and gather detailed information at www.Biltmore.com., or call Biltmore information, 800-411-3812.

393.6 The North Carolina Arboretum 🚹 🚻 ♿

The North Carolina Arboretum is a 434-acre public garden and trail system located within the Bent Creek Experimental forest. This is a must see for any gardener or horticulturist and offers more of an intimate experience than the usual Parkway grand-scenic views. Ten miles of hiking and biking trails (some multi-use) offer diversity, but the nearby Pisgah area trails are worth the extra drive if hiking is your goal. The real draws are the gardens, and in April and early May, the National Native Azalea Repository, where 13 of the 16 species of native flame azaleas are featured.

Don't miss the quilt garden. A pattern is chosen from a traditional mountain quilt and replicated in the garden using seasonal plants and flowers. An elevated archway allows a more aerial view of the pattern. The Bonsai Exhibition Garden presents a botanically diverse bonsai collection of over 100 plants, many of which are native to the Blue Ridge region.

Frederick Law Olmsted, our nation's father of landscape architecture envisioned such a place almost a century ago. It now stands as an ongoing living, working facility carrying out the vision that he passed on to generations of professional and amateur landscape designers and gardeners. Olmsted was directly responsible for designing the Biltmore Estate grounds, New York City's Central Park, and those of the U.S. Capitol, among others. The ripple effect of his work and thought is found throughout the nation and the Blue Ridge Parkway.

LEFT: An elevated view of a design in the quilt garden of sage, kale and Carolina mum.

RIGHT: A large stand of flame azalea at Engine Gap (off-Parkway, Roan Mountain).

A wide variety of classes and workshops are taught by the staff and other visiting experts. Educational programs target all ages and range from bonsai demonstrations to nature walks. You can tour at your own pace with a map and pamphlet or take a Segway™ tour which is offered twice a day at 10 AM and 2 PM, except Sundays. A café and two gift shops are on site. There is a modest parking fee in lieu of an entry fee. The Arboretum grounds open from 8 AM to 9 PM, April to October, and 8 AM to 7 PM, November to March, with shorter hours for the Education Center and other buildings.

Leashed pets are permitted and doggie waste bags are available on site. The Arboretum's Education Center, Greenhouse and gardens are wheelchair accessible and wheelchairs are available for visitors to borrow. Phone 828-665-2492 or visit www.ncarboretum.org. for more details and to inquire about what's blooming.

Opening spread: Muhli grass and goldenrod glow in soft evening light at the Arboretum.

BELOW: Spicebush swallowtail nectars happily on the N.C. Arboretum grounds.

"...We were alarmed with apprehension of the hill being set on fire. This is certainly the most gay and brilliant flowering shrub yet known." William Bartram.

Well, OK! Speech was flowery then too, and prone to hyperbole, but the bright orange flame azalea, when blooming in a dense stand, is a sight to see. The National Native Azalea Repository nurtures 13 of the 16 native azalea species. Ten of these are found in the southern Appalachians, nine in North Carolina. The majority of the species are found within 100 miles of the Arboretum, many along the Parkway itself, including the rare pinkshell azalea (*R. vaseyi*), which is native to only a few counties in Western North Carolina. You can witness its beautiful pink blooms in late May along the Blue Ridge Parkway from the Waterrock Knob area to the Mount Pisgah area, at Linville Gorge and Grandfather Mountain. You will find individual plants and small colonies throughout the Parkway. To see large stands of flame azaleas you will have to venture off-Parkway to Engine Gap at Roan Mountain, or to Gregory or Andrews Balds in the Great Smokies. Each of those locations involves hiking to destination.

LAND *of* MILK *and* HONEY

10

PISGAH
GRAVEYARD FIELDS

MP 407 - 431

On Parkway

Mount Pisgah
Looking Glass Rock
Graveyard Fields
Devil's Courthouse
Cowee Mountains Overlook
Richland Balsam

Off Parkway

Cradle *of* Forestry
Looking Glass Creek *and* Falls
Black Balsam Area
Shining Rock Wilderness

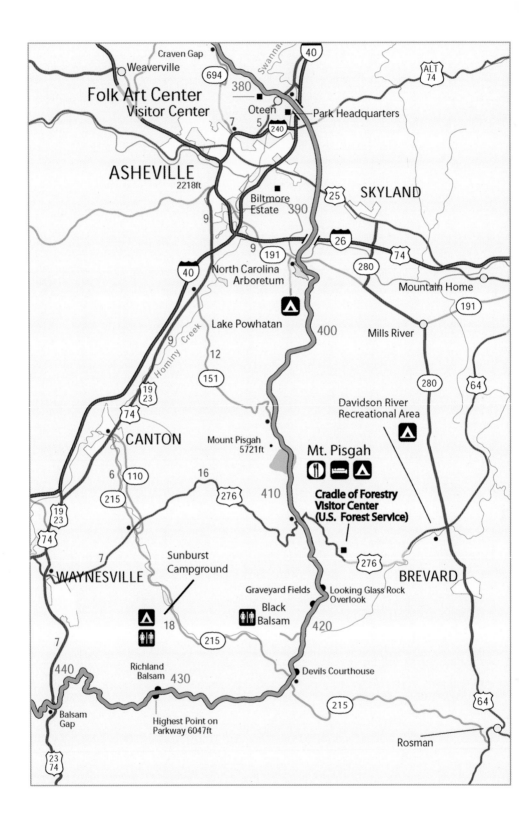

MP	POINT OF INTEREST	FEATURES
407.7	Mt. Pisgah trail	Hiking trail to summit
408.6	Pisgah Inn	Lodging, dining, gift shop, scenic views
exit 412	Cradle of Forestry Visitor Center	Exhibits, hiking trails, historic buildings, interpretive programs
exit 412	Sliding Rock	Swimming in season, scenery
exit 412	Looking Glass Falls	Roadside Waterfall
413	Pounding Mill Overlook	Scenic views
418.8	Graveyard Fields	Scenic views, hiking
420.2	Black Balsam area — Shining Rock Wilderness trailhead, Art Loeb Trail to Black Balsam Knob and Tennent Mt.	Scenic hikes, wilderness hiking, campground, restrooms
422	Devil's Courthouse	Short hiking trail to summit views
exit 423	NC 215— north to Waynesville and south to Brevard	Scenic drive with two roadside waterfalls northbound, icicles southbound in winter
425	Middle Prong Wilderness access at Rough Butt Bald Overlook	Wilderness hiking
430.7	Cowee Mountains Overlook	Scenic views
431.4	Richland Balsam	Highest elevation on the Parkway, nearby trailhead to summit

MP	LODGING AND DINING	MP	CAMPING
388.8	U.S. 25— Lodging, three miles north; dining, 1 mile either way	408.6	Mt. Pisgah Campground a BRP campground, seasonal
393.6	NC 191—about two miles north	412	U.S. 276— East about 20 miles Davidson River, USFS, year round
408.6	Pisgah Inn	exit 423	Sunburst CG NC 215 about nine miles north, USFS, seasonal

MP	GASOLINE		HOSPITAL
388.8	U.S. 25 —1.5 miles north, one-half mile south	388.8	**Memorial Mission Hospital** 828- 213-1111 about 4 miles north of Parkway on U.S. 25
393.6	NC 191—about 2 miles north	412	U.S. 276 (E) to U.S. 64 (W) to Brevard - **Transylvania Community Hospital** 828-883-5243
412	U.S. 276, east to Brevard about 25 miles, and west towards Waynesville, about 20 miles	443	U.S. 74 (W) about 12 miles Waynesville - **Haywood Regional Medical Center** 828-452-8110
423	NC 215 —about 15 miles north		
443	U.S.— 74 about 4 miles west towards Waynesville		

The rising sun peaks over the ridges looking down at Mills River Valley between Asheville and Mount Pisgah.

OVERVIEW

Leaving Asheville, head south to more North Carolina high country, soon dominated by Mt. Pisgah. *Elseetoss* to the Cherokee, accounts vary as to who renamed the peak, but the first published reference to it by its new name reportedly appeared in 1808. James Hall, an army chaplain in 1776, and George Newton, an Asheville Presbyterian minister in the late 1700s are both credited with renaming the mountain. The rich fertile valley of the French Broad River surrounded by the high peaks of the Mount Pisgah area likely struck both men as resembling the Biblical land of milk and honey; the peak was renamed after that fabled mountain. George Vanderbilt also admired this high country, so much in fact that he bought a lot of it, about 125,000 acres. The Mount Pisgah area in particular was dear to his heart and home to his original mountain retreat, as well as the nation's first forestry school. Today you can enjoy the outstanding scenery and the clean mountain air without being a high roller on George's restricted guest list. This chapter is detail intense due to the many scenic features and recreational opportunities in the surrounding Pisgah National Forest.

Gas up before you get on the Parkway, there aren't any fueling options close by. Pisgah Inn has a wonderful restaurant in season (spring summer, and fall) with comfortable lodging; the campground there is the other nearby overnight option. You can stay the night in Asheville, Brevard, or Waynesville or camp at Davidson River and still easily enjoy this area if a night in the high country isn't in the cards for you.

Climb steadily, leave the banks of the French Broad River in Asheville and pass several overlooks that offer views of the valleys and ridges to the south and east. Photographers and sunrise lovers who have limited time can make a quick foray up the Parkway for daybreak and be back in town in time for breakfast. Continue on to the 407 mark to the Mt. Pisgah area. As you near the Inn, visit the Mt. Pisgah Parking area and the trailhead for the short but steep climb to the summit. A picnic area is another quarter mile down the road soon followed by the Pisgah Inn and Mt. Pisgah Campground, MP 408.6. The Inn has a superb restaurant that serves three meals a day and can make a picnic lunch for you and has comfortable accommodations to boot. The campground is easy walking distance from the Inn for those who are traveling in self contained mode.

Three miles south at MP 412, find the intersection of U.S. 276 at Wagon Road Gap. U.S. 276 takes you four miles east to the Cradle of Forestry in America Forest Discovery Center with its many exhibits, trails, and interpretive sites. Continue towards Brevard to the scenic Looking Glass Creek, Sliding Rock (a Forest Service day use facility and swimming hole), Looking Glass Falls, the Davidson River area and Brevard itself. Brevard can be a great hub from which to explore this stretch of the Parkway as well as the many off-Parkway waterfalls in the area. There is so much to see in this area, it's a slippery slope upon which to step.

To the west, 276 takes you to Waynesville, NC and the I-40 corridor. U.S. 276 is almost always open in the winter offering access to the high country for hiking, cross country skiing, sledding and snow ball fights. Driving mountain roads in snowy icy conditions is a major undertaking; do so with extreme caution! You will need more than a cell phone for a back up plan in event of a mishap.

Another mile further brings you to Pounding Mill Overlook, MP 413, one of the Parkway's best scenic overlooks. For the next five miles, you will have overlooks with various views of Looking Glass Rock's stony face.

Graveyard Fields with its scenic overlooks and hiking trails waits at MP 418.8. One and one-half miles further brings you to Forest Road 816, a one-mile spur road leading to the Black Balsam Area with high country trailheads to Shining Rock Wilderness, Black Balsam Knob

Alpenglow lights the clouds over the Parkway at Cowee Mountain Overlook MP 430.7

and Tennent Mountain, among others. You will find rest rooms (modern "vault toilets") at road's end, and a kiosk with a trail map at the trailhead.

Devil's Courthouse comes at MP 422, offering a short but steep trail to a lofty observation area. Beech Gap at MP 423 allows Parkway access via NC 215 from Waynesville and Brevard. Descend NC 215 about two miles to the north for scenic views of Bubbling Springs Falls, which at the peak of fall color is one of most appealing scenes anywhere in the entire nation. Further down is a roadside view of an upper branch of the West Fork of the Pigeon River which tumbles out of the Middle Prong Wilderness Area. Continue to Waynesville. To the east of the Parkway lies U.S. 64 leading to Brevard, Cashiers and Highlands.

Further on past several overlooks, all offering ethereal views, you will reach Buckeye Gap and the Rough Butt Bald Overlook, MP 425. Across the Parkway is an obscure trailhead leading into the Middle Prong Wilderness. It's about five miles further southbound to the Cowee Mountains Overlook which is another top Parkway vista. Six miles of additional scenery gets you to the Richland

The kitchen hearth in the old Ranger's residence periodically comes to life with interpretive staff at the Forest Discovery Center.

Balsam Overlook, the Blue Ridge Parkway high point at 6,053 feet. From here you will descend towards Balsam Gap and U.S. 23-74, with access to Waynesville and Sylva NC and our final segment of the Parkway.

407.7 Mt. Pisgah Trail (4,995)

Coming from Asheville, drive through the Buck Springs Tunnel, turn into the large overlook to your left and follow the winding road to the end of the parking area. The trailhead is at the end of the parking area. In little over one mile the trail gains 762 feet elevation, much of it in the final half. Yep, starts out mellow, and gets steeper. The trail leads through wooded high altitude environs to the summit (5,721 feet) observation tower and excellent views including the most attractive face of Cold Mountain to the northwest. The gnarled and twisted trees near the summit bear living testimony to the harsh windy conditions at this elevation. Atop this peak is a 339-foot tall tower and broadcasting antenna for local TV and radio stations in nearby Asheville. The tower and similar structures are exempt from the North Carolina Ridge Law, however they are no less obtrusive. Hopefully an effective but less visible alternate location can be found. Allow at least one hour to hike to the top, enjoy the views, and return.

408.6 Pisgah Inn

This is the perfect high country hub for visiting this part of the Parkway, and is a stop over for many folks just passing through. Reservations for lodging are essential; also, plan to get there early for dinner before the specials run out. Breakfast is an excellent country style affair; lunch and dinner range from basic to upscale. Wine and beer are served. The large gift shop has an extensive inventory of Parkway related publications and crafts. There are excellent views from the grounds. The adjacent campground rarely fills to capacity, but call ahead if you plan to stay over a busy holiday weekend. For reservations at the Inn, or for possible last minute cancellations, call 828-235-8228. You can also visit on the web at www.pisgahinn.com. The Inn is closed in the winter.

Cradle of Forestry
Looking Glass Falls

🚶 ⓘ 🍴 🚻

Leaving the Parkway, take U.S. 276 east and descend steeply through a visually exciting hardwood forest for four miles to the Forest Discovery Center at the Cradle of Forestry. This Forest Service facility, located at the site of Dr. Schenck's original forestry school, commemorates the beginning of forestry science in this country. George Vanderbilt bought much of the surrounding Pisgah National Forest lands in the late 1800's. The land had been sorely abused and needed rehabilitation. Gifford Pinchot became his first forest manager and later became the first chief of the U.S. Forest Service. He was followed here by a German forester, Dr. Carl Schenck, who trained many early foresters in the fledgling discipline.

You will find an excellent film detailing that history and more, as well as many exhibits designed to educate and entertain the young and old alike. The Forest Discovery Center also features a gift shop and café. The mile-long, paved Biltmore Campus Trail is wheelchair accessible and built to ADA standards; you might need some assistance for a few steeper pitches. This trail passes several of the original structures, some in their original locations, including vintage ranger cabins. One was moved to protect it from vandalism after others were sadly torched. Interpretive staff add a living history touch when volunteers are available. The center is open seasonally from April to November. Call 828-877-3130 for additional information or visit www.cradleofforestry.org.

Allow at least two hours to see the film clip, visit the facility and tour the Biltmore Campus Trail, longer to take in the other trails or photograph.

ABOVE: Prussian style detail on an original Ranger Cabin along the Biltmore Campus Trail at the Forest Discovery Center.

RIGHT: Fire cherry adds a splash of fall color along Looking Glass Creek below Sliding Rock.

Looking Glass Falls is visible from the roadside, and you can photograph it from a number of angles. Stream flow is usually low enough to allow a downstream perspective in mid stream. Get far enough downstream so that spray doesn't drench your lens.

Follow U.S. 276 east to Sliding Rock, a recreational day use facility. Here a large sloping rock shelf terminates in a 7-foot deep plunge pool. The rock is slicker than it looks, take care to keep "sliders" from becoming "rockets." This is a very popular swimming hole and the area is quite scenic in the bargain. Photographers will enjoy the creek below the recreational area and it's only a short roadside walk.

Continue on to Looking Glass Falls, an abrupt drop on Looking Glass Creek which you have been following. The large roadside parking area and viewing platform have recently been updated. Photographers will find additional compositions further downstream from waters edge. From here it's a short distance to the Davidson River Recreation Area

and fish hatchery, campground and on to Brevard.

If you tour the Discovery Center, drive down to follow Looking Glass Creek and spend a few minutes at the Falls, you could easily spend three hours or more. From the Falls, Brevard is another 15 minutes or so if you are getting hungry or need gas.

413 Pounding Mill Overlook (4,700)

This large overlook is one of the most impressive on the entire Parkway and gives probably the most photogenic views of Looking Glass Rock.

Photo Notes

Get to Pounding Mill Overlook early, 30 minutes before sunrise if you can. The predawn light show is unpredictable, but you may be rewarded with fiery skies and fog in the valley. Breezes start stirring a few minutes after the sun breaks the horizon. This scene can be attractive until midmorning, and again in the afternoon.

LEFT AND OPENING SPREAD: Looking Glass Rock from Pounding Mill Overlook.

Photographers will find this one of the best dawn locations in the area, and evening light can provide superb memories as well. Morning fog often layers in the valley below and can completely obscure Looking Glass Rock in certain conditions. If that happens, and you have time, wait to see the changing kaleidoscope as the fog breaks and lifts. Unfortunately no one can reliably predict how long that might take; sometimes less than an hour, sometimes all day.

418.8 Graveyard Fields (5,120) 🚶

The Graveyard Fields area is not a place to rush through and you should plan your day's journey accordingly. In all seasons, the Graveyard Fields area is enchanting—early May will bring both sarvis and maple blooms, early June sees Catawba rhododendron and mountain laurel, mid-summer brings a profusion of turks cap lily to the flanks of Tennent Mountain with its carpet of mountain oat grass; September brings forth a pro-

fusion of goldenrod and early October finishes the show with brilliant fall color. Second Falls on the Yellowstone Prong is a short walk from the parking area, and the climb to Black Balsam Knob and Tennent Mountain is short from nearby Black Balsam. If you are not a hiker of any sort, the views of Second Falls and the valley below as you approach the parking area will catch your eye and the different views from the large parking area will keep you occupied for quite some time. Look for breaking sunbeams here, one or two hours before sunset.

Different views of Second Falls. Preceding spread shows the valley as seen from the road as you approach Graveyard Fields from the north. Spring color rivals fall for a few days in early May. The above view is near the observation deck at the base of the falls.

Twenty years of continuous logging after the turn of the century removed vast stands of red spruce, Fraser fir, eastern hemlocks and various hardwoods. Common practice of the day left large heaps of waste (slash) laying around after the trees were harvested. A 1925 wildfire burned over 20,000 acres in three days, almost sterilizing the soil. Regrowth was slow until a second fire occurred in 1942. The many charred stumps were reminiscent of the tombstones in a graveyard, hence the name.

A large sign at the northerly trailhead details the various Graveyard Fields trails. The option for creating loops allows you to tear off only as much as you can chew. The Graveyard Fields Trail makes a 3.2-mile loop that can take you all the way to the upper falls if you have

the time, but most visitors take the short 0.3-mile out-and-back route to Second Falls, which is much closer, larger and more scenic.

From the parking area descend the steep steps through a rhododendron tunnel to creek side at 0.2 miles, cross the wooden bridge and bear to your right for another couple of hundred yards then descend a set of wooden stairs to a large observation platform below the falls. In summer this is a popular sunbathing spot. Allow at least 45 minutes to see the falls.

The trail continues further to a set of lower falls which are situated in a deep ravine and are almost inaccessible. Fishing is said to be fair for small, up to 8-inch trout in Yellowstone Prong. The Graveyard Ridge Trail provides access to the Art Loeb Trail and the Mountains-to-Sea Trail on the ridges high above the valley floor, and could be of interest to the serious hiker. That's the connector to the Ivestor Gap area and Black Balsam Knob areas from the valley floor.

A less obvious second trailhead waits at the southerly end of the parking area and closes the loop of the Graveyard Fields Trail. This less steep descent (or ascent) obviates the need to retrace your steps if you chose to hike the entire loop. More rhododendron tunnels lead to the flat, somewhat boggy, valley floor before continuing on to Upper Falls. You can make a return loop after you cross the creek for about a 2-mile jaunt, with a steeper final quarter mile.

PHOTO NOTES

The preceding abbreviated almanac gives you a rough idea of what seasonal attractions to expect. Images from the roadside overlooking the valley and Second Falls can be stunning. That scene is backlighted in mid-to-late afternoon. Shadows will advance into the composition as the afternoon wears on — it's not a last light place. This location gets early morning light, though not first light. Dramatic clouds can add interest and afternoon sunbeams are dramatic here.

The falls are very photogenic from close up as well. Follow the quarter-mile trail to the observation deck. Many additional compositions await from the shoreline and mid-stream. The higher ridges and peaks to the west limit sunset options, but you can reach any of several evening light vantage points down Parkway (south) from here. This place "rocks" in the fog, i.e. low lying clouds as seen from lower elevations.

420.2 Black Balsam

Forest Road 816 leaves the Parkway to a high country trailhead locally known as Black Balsam, with trails leading to many destinations — this is Grand Central Station for high-country hiking. "Black Balsam" is frequently used to refer to the general area as distinct from "Graveyard Fields" and I have used it in that context.

This is an off-Parkway detour for hikers; if that's not for you, you can safely pass this by and drive on down the road. If you have any interest in stretching your legs, this detour is for you. Black Balsam also has the only area restrooms for those needing to answer a nature call.

The large parking area at the end of the road is the staging zone for most of the high country hikes. There are two modern, non-flush, non-stinky, "vault toilets" in the parking area. The wide trail heading north is your ticket to the Shining Rock Wilderness and a loop that connects to Graveyard Fields, Black Balsam Knob and Tennent Mountain on the ridge line above you to the east.

This trail is an old roadbed and is open to 4WD vehicles from mid-August until hunting season ends. Walk the road once to see whose vehicle you want to take on that ride—not mine!! Hard core wilderness lovers won't like the idea of walking on a road and having some 4x4 break the wilderness spell isn't my cup of tea either. However, the only time I have actually seen vehicles on it, was when a group of bear hunters passed through while I was in the parking area having a late dinner.

CLOCKWISE FROM LEFT: Goldenrod on Black Balsam Knob at sunrise, Shining Rock Summit in evening light, sunrise near Ivestor Gap in early October.

SHINING ROCK - BLACK BALSAM TRAILS

BLACK BALSAM KNOB - TENNENT MOUNTAIN

From the Parkway, look for an obvious parking area in 0.6 miles. Enter the dark woods to your right (the Mountains-to-Sea Trail crosses south on your left) and bear left on the Art Loeb Trail. A couple of minutes in the thick dark regrowth will bring you out to the open flanks of Black Balsam Knob. Ascend to the summit (6,214) in maybe 10-15 minutes to 360-degree views of the surrounding area. There is a profusion of goldenrod in late August and early September and a large colony of turks cap lily in mid-summer. Fabulous rock formations that look like lava flows adorn the crest. Continue 10 more minutes on to the summit of Tennent Mountain (6,040) with its wide-open feel and carpets of mountain oat grass waving softly in the faintest breeze. Retrace your steps, or continue to Ivestor Gap where you can loop back to the Graveyard Fields area on the Graveyard Ridge Trail. You could also return to Black Balsam Parking Area via the Investor Gap Trail and hoof it another 0.4 miles along the road your car. Allow at least one hour to go out and back.

IVESTOR GAP

The trailhead is at the northerly end of the parking area, and is a nearly level road for the two miles it takes to get to the gap. A quarter-mile closer is a small spring with a rubber collecting pipe. Treat this water, but it tastes wonderfully fresh. A side trail leads over a small knob festooned with young evergreens that makes an excellent campsite. Another spring flows from the west face of the knob across the trail. Extensive fields of blueberry cover the hillsides and put on their fall hues in late September. Return the way you came, loop back on the Art Loeb, or continue on to Shining Rock. Allow at least one hour each way to Ivestor Gap.

SHINING ROCK

Shining Rock entices hikers to add some additional mileage to the outing. From Ivestor Gap, two more relatively level miles brings you to Shining Rock Gap where multiple trails seem to intersect. The somewhat obscure spur leading to Shining Rock summit (6,040) is ahead through the trees and campsites slightly to your left. The Little East Fork trail contours left, bypassing the summit. Ascend to the top through trees and campsites to scramble up the white quartz formation. Return the way you came, being wary of false leads. A little noticed trail comes in behind you as you near the Gap, bear to the left at this fork on your way back to follow your bread crumbs to the parking area. The trail is a bit stony with some ankle twisters, so be mindful, but its otherwise an easy hike. The intrepid can continue on to Cold Mountain for a 16-mile round trip. Allow at least two hours each way from Black Balsam parking area to Shining Rock, plus additional time to soak it all in.

There are enough hiking options in this area to fill a small book, well beyond the scope of this one. The trail to Sam Knob and Flat Laurel Creek are also worthy of consideration. The three hikes listed in the sidebar vary in length and difficulty. All offer outstanding scenery and have much photographic potential. The Shining Rock area is very popular and can be crowded on weekends and holidays. If solitude is important to you, consider the adjacent Middle Prong Wilderness.

422	**Devil's Courthouse (5,462)** 🚶

This overlook offers views of the rocky face of Devil's Courthouse and a short but steep trail leading to the summit with expansive views of the Piedmont to the south. According to Cherokee legend an evil spirit held court here, passing judgment on those lacking a warrior's courage. The short hike to the summit may pass judgment on your heart and lungs; be advised it's a mini stress test all its own. The trail passes through more rhododendron tunnels amidst the skeletons

of Fraser firs, and the remaining spruce trees. This is also home to the endangered northern flying squirrel, and a prime location for observing the annual hawk migration in late September.

exit 423	**Scenic Detour N.C. 215**

This crossing road not only affords egress and ingress to the Parkway, it leads to more scenic splendor. If you haven't already reached sensory overload take a short side trip down this steep winding road, you will be glad you did. The road cleaves two wilderness areas; to the east the recently mentioned Shining Rock, and to the west the unheralded and lightly visited Middle Prong Wilderness. Soon after descending NC 215 to the north, you will pass a trailhead for the Mountains-to-Sea Trail that leads to Sam Knob to the east, and eventually to Mount Hardy in Middle Prong Wilderness to the west. About two miles down from the Parkway you will pass a gravel pullout to your right with views of a waterfall across the way. This cascade is Bubbling Springs Falls whose source is

BELOW: A splendid roadside cascade tumbles out of Middle Prong Wilderness, still proud following the storms. **ABOVE RIGHT:** Roadside view of Bubbling Springs Falls in early October.

on the flanks of Sam Knob above. This scene in full fall color is a wonder to behold. Peak color doesn't last long at this scene, sometimes only a day or two, before some rogue storm blows it all off. It is always worth the short detour to check it out. A couple of miles further down the road is an unnamed branch of the West Fork of the Pigeon River. NC 215 crosses it, and there is a convenient pull off to the left that will hold three or four vehicles. Sunburst campground is about five miles further down the road.

This streambed, the West Fork of the Pigeon River, and many other high mountain streams were altered for our lifetimes by the flood waters of Hurricanes Frances and Ivan in 2004. The bare bones of this cascade remain, but the "trim," that is to say the foliage growing alongside, will take years to recover. It is a gorgeous place still, and nature has a way of healing the land after a storm. Its definitely worth the couple of added miles descent to check it out. Continue on 215 to connect to U.S. 276 to Waynesville

or return to the Parkway. Down the other side of the Parkway headed south on NC 215 is a large rock walled seep, home to lichen and salamanders, and in the dead of winter, host to fantastic icicle formations. Should you have a winter Parkway adventure, check it out.

Back on the Parkway headed south, plan to stop frequently to enjoy the many scenic overlooks. While all are variations on a theme, each offers a different view of the ridges and valleys below. Be careful leaving and entering traffic.

425 Middle Prong Wilderness

The Rough Butt Bald Overlook, MP 425 (5,300), offers views though better ones surround it. It is, however, a convenient access to the Middle Prong Wilderness, whose miles of hiking trails offer a less crowded alternative to the immensely popular Shining Rock Wilderness.

The summer sun sets far to the right (northwest) and is more to the southwest (your left) in the spring and fall. This is the premier sunset location on this stretch of the Parkway. The following spread is from the same location in October.

Through the roadside forest across from the south end of the parking area is an obscure trail leading into the wilderness. In a couple of hundred yards you will come to an intersection with the Mountains-to-Sea Trail. Hiking to the right will take you in about one mile of gentle trail to an open area with a high grassy knob to the north, and the untracked flanks of Mount Hardy to the south. The usual spring wildflowers make these trails special in early-to-mid May. A short spin on this trail probably won't get you lost, but its easy to get turned around in the wild. Take a map and compass.

430.7 Cowee Mountains Overlook (5,960)

This scene invites, no demands, hyperbole. The distant stacked ridges serve up the quintessential Blue Ridge Mountain view. Spring and fall hues change the mood, and summer wildflowers add a color accent along the fringe of the overlook. This is one of the Parkway's finest views, a MUST STOP vista. This is also one of the best locations to watch sunset over those stacked ridges beyond. You can usually get to Waynesville or Pisgah Inn for dinner.

Photo Notes

The stretch of Parkway from Cowee Mountains Overlook to Beech Gap is fantastically scenic with endless photo opportunities. Sunrise and sunset azimuths vary by time of year and bend in the road. You will have cross light or the sun in your frame depending on location and season. The summer sun sets more to the northwest and can sneak out of view from many vantage points, only to return in the fall.

You will find great comps near the Herrin Knob Overlook, MP 424.4 , and the adjacent ridges and curves. Cowee is always superb. Look for sunbeams breaking through broken clouds in late afternoon, a couple of hours before sunset. In the fall, you can easily photograph sunset and have a leisurely drive to dinner. The late-setting summer sun dictates having an early dinner beforehand, or having something with you.

Autumn sunset near Herrin Knob Overlook at MP 424.4. A setting summer sun would swing out of view to the right from this location.

431.4 Richland Balsam (6,053)

A trail to the 6,410 foot high summit originates at the Haywood Jackson Overlook 0.4 miles to the north. This is an out-and-back trail almost 1.5 miles in length, through now familiar boreal forest with seasonal wildflowers and interpretive information regarding the plight of the spruce-fir ecosystem. In case you missed it, here is another opportunity to become educated about the devastation wrought by the Balsam Woolly Adelgid that decimated the Fraser (a.k.a. balsam)

fir forest in the 1960s and '70s and unfortunately hasn't loosened its death grip. The views from the overlook itself aren't particularly exciting but it's a stopover that most folks don't miss. There is a large commemorative sign naming the overlook and its prominent elevation that has figured in many vacation portfolios.

From here you will descend towards Balsam Gap at MP 443.1, and its intersection with U.S. 23-74. This provides access to Waynesville and Sylva N.C., as well as being a gateway to your final segment of the Parkway.

the *the* LAST THIRTY MILES

MP 439 - 469

Waterrock Knob

Soco Gap

Balsam Mountain Road
(Spur Road to Great Smokies)

Oconaluftee Mountain Farm Museum
(Great Smoky Mountains National Park)

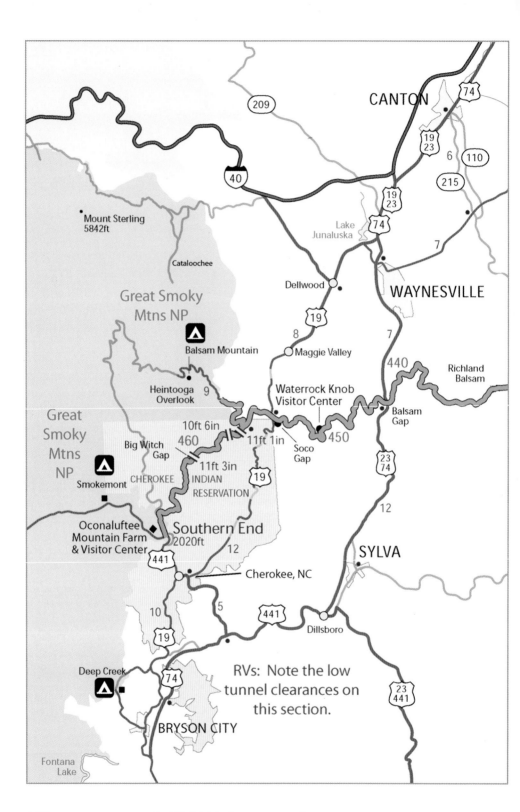

Above: A misty summer sunset glows as seen from Woolyback Overlook, MP 452.3.
Opening spread: Twilight's purple hues lend new meaning to the phrase "purple mountains majesty" as seen from the Waterrock Knob Trail, MP 451.

RVs NOTE LOW TUNNEL CLEARANCE IN THIS SECTION OF THE PARKWAY.

MP	POINT OF INTEREST	FEATURES
451	Waterrock Knob	Scenic views, hiking trail, visitor center, restrooms
455	Soco Gap	Scenic views, intersection U.S. 19 to Maggie Valley and Cherokee
458.2	Heintooga Ridge Road	Spur road to Great Smoky Mtns. NP, scenic views, hiking, Balsam Mtn. campground
469	End Blue Ridge Parkway, enter Great Smoky Mountains National Park	Oconaluftee Mountain Farm Museum, visitor center, U.S. 441 to Cherokee and Gatlinburg, TN.

MP	LODGING, DINING & GAS	MP	CAMPING
443	U.S. 74 — 8 miles west to Waynesville	458.2	Balsam Mtn CG (Smokies) Mile High CG (commercial)
455	U.S. 19 — 3 miles north to Maggie Valley	**MP**	**HOSPITAL**
469	U.S. 441 — 2 miles south to Cherokee	443	U.S. 74 — about 12 miles west **Haywood Regional Medical Center** 828-452-8110 Waynesville

Sunbeams break through the clouds over spring blooming sarvis trees near Waterrock Knob

OVERVIEW

The Parkway starts out with a bang at MP 6.0 with a very interesting living history display and progresses quickly into high mountain scenery coursing through Virginia's wild mountains. In its final thirty miles, the Parkway descends from the North Carolina heights to the banks of the Oconaluftee River and Great Smoky Mountains National Park. There isn't anything special about the number "thirty," it just seemed to work out that way when writing this book.

This section starts at Balsam Gap, (3,370) MP 443, winds around over Waterrock Knob with its fabulous views, descends to Soco Gap and makes a final dash towards its rendezvous with the Smokies. You could easily have started the day in Asheville or Brevard if you were simply driving and stopping at some overlooks. If you were lucky and had reservations, or a last minute cancellation, you spent the night at the Pisgah Inn. Waynesville has been attracting high country travelers for many years, as has Maggie Valley, near Soco Gap. Of course, you could be starting a Parkway trip from the southern end, having stayed in Cherokee, or even in Tennessee.

This section is light on hiking, but strong on scenic views, as it follows the high ridges of the Plott Balsams, another sub range of the Blue Ridge Mountains. The Plott Balsams and the Great Balsam Mountains were named for the thick growth of Fraser fir trees, also known as "balsam" firs, for the sap they extruded. The Plott Balsams were named for the Amos Plott family, one of the area's first settlers.

Climb steeply from Balsam Gap to the high reaches of Waterrock Knob Overlook (6,047) and summit (6,292), at MP 451, a gain of almost 3,000 vertical feet in a short eight miles. This change in elevation can often allow you to experience two different seasons in a short 20 minutes, along with the ever-present fine mountain scenery. You will find a seasonal visitor center with views, restrooms and a hiking trail. As you descend from Waterrock Knob, you will pass more overlooks, all of which serve up superb mountain vistas and present views of the setting sun to the west. Soco Gap, MP 455, sees the crossing of U.S. 19 to Cherokee, Maggie Valley and Waynesville. Soco Gap is exceptionally scenic and worthy of a stop on its own.

Drive on to Wolf Laurel Gap at MP 458.2 and the Heintooga Ridge Road that exits the Parkway to enter Great Smoky Mountains National Park. This road leads to additional views, hiking trails and Balsam Mountain Campground at 5,310 elevation. From Wolf Laurel Gap it's a scenic 11-mile descent to the banks of the Oconaluftee River and the southern end of the Parkway.

There is symmetry of sorts. The living history display that mirrors Humpback Rocks is actually in the Smokies itself, but only a quarter mile from the "469" milestone on the Blue Ridge Parkway. Technically in a different park, it's also part of YOUR national park system. So, for the sake of said symmetry and informing you, the reader, I included the Oconaluftee Mountain Farm Museum.

Exfoliating rock shards spring forth like bare bones of the earth near Waterrock Knob.

451 Waterrock Knob (6,047) 🅿 🚻 🚶

Waterrock Knob at 6,292 feet elevation is the high point in the Plott Balsam Range, a subunit of the Blue Ridge Mountains, and the high point on this stretch of the Parkway. It can be drizzling in the valley below while thick frost is forming at these heights — spring is often well underway in the valleys below while the Knob is still firmly in winter's icy grip.

The short spur from the Parkway climbs to a very large parking area, visitor center and trailhead for the summit jaunt. The visitor center is open seasonally and the large parking area is a local favorite to hang out in the cool mountain air and watch the sun go down. Hungry sunset

Hoar frost, aka rime ice forms on exposed surfaces whenever the temperature drops below freezing inside a cloud. You will find this happens often at higher elevations when cold fronts move through. Often the pavement is dry when this happens so the Parkway stays open allowing you to enjoy a winter wonderland.

This delightful scene was near the View Yellow Face Overlook, MP 450.

FOLLOWING SPREAD: The gorgeous pastels of spring adorn the mountainside at Soco Gap, MP 455.

watchers take comfort; Maggie Valley is but a few short miles away, easily within reach for a relaxed dinner.

The trailhead is near the apex of the parking area and climbs steeply before reaching a briefly level shelf; this gives a bit of breather before the final push to the top. It's a little over one-half mile to the top, and the elevation may have you huffing and puffing. You are higher here than in Denver, so take it a bit slower if you need to.

Be sure to pull over often between here and Soco Gap. Each overlook has its own special personality and will well reward your stop.

455 Soco Gap (4,340)

Soco Gap is a crossroads for U.S. 19, leading to Cherokee, Maggie Valley and Waynesville. Its easy just to blow through here en-route to something down the road, but I encourage you to pull over for little while to enjoy this enchanting place. There are several incredible oaks here that have seen many ages pass and the mountainsides covered in soft spring pastels in mid-May are among the best anywhere. Fall color peaks here around mid-October, and U.S. 19 is usually open in winter, reopening soon after major

Dried summer grasses grace a roadside scene below Waterrock Knob.

storms. This gives you a winter fun option if skiing at nearby Cataloochee isn't your idea of grins. Through Maggie, it's only 14 miles to exit #20 at I-40.

| exit 458.2 | Heintooga Ridge Road △ 🚶 🚹🚺 |

Exit the Parkway at Wolf Laurel Gap to follow this road leading into Great Smoky Mountains National Park. After 3.5 miles you will leave the Blue Ridge Parkway and enter the Smokies, the distinction easily being lost. The pavement ends eight miles from Wolf Laurel Gap at Heintooga picnic area and Balsam Mountain campground. From the end of the pavement you can descend (when open) the unpaved Balsam Mountain Road to the Cherokee area; otherwise, retrace your steps back to the Parkway.

There is a private campground one mile from Wolf Laurel Gap in addition to Balsam Mountain campground at pavement's end. You will find several hiking options once you enter the Smokies; one of the best area hikes for late spring wildflowers is close by, described next.

The Flat Creek Trail offers a profusion of wildflowers including carpets of fringed phacelia in early May. If the Heintooga Ridge Road is not yet open for the season, it's a short walk of less than one mile from the locked gate to the trailhead which is

The gentle Flat Creek Trail is a wildflower lover's gift in early May.

signed on your left. If the gate is open, it's a hair over five miles from where you turned off the Parkway. As soon as you leave the trailhead, the flowers are at your feet; you will see the best displays in the first mile. The luxuriant growth of spring wildflowers is breathtaking. Non-hikers will find excellent roadside displays of spring beauties and other seasonal favorites. Retrace your tracks or continue on another two miles to the Heintooga picnic area.

exit 469

Oconaluftee Mountain Farm Museum

Oconaluftee visitor center is adjacent to this fully restored homestead, complete with plowed corn rows and fences. The Davis House is a fine example of period architecture. You will notice similarities between this exhibit and the one at Humpback Rocks.

One-half mile further up the road is Mingus Mill. This fully operational scenic mill operates from spring to fall, and sells authentic stone ground cornmeal. The inner workings of the mill are visible on the self guided tour. If you are lucky, you will find the miller at work who can tell many tales of mountain life in the "old days." Allow at least one hour for the Mountain Farm and visitor center, and 30 minutes for Mingus Mill.

For current information, call the visitor center at 828-497-1900.

ABOVE RIGHT: Davis House in early April with forsythia in bloom.
LOWER RIGHT: The sluiceway and Mingus Mill.

THE
CHALLENGE AHEAD

A proliferation of vacation home construction in the North Carolina mountains threatens Parkway views. Here a new home is perched above the Parkway below.

THE ENEMY WITHIN

The Parkway and the lands that surround it are under constant pressure from many different threats. Insect pests and industrial pollutants have combined to visibly change the landscape in the Virginia and North Carolina mountains. That in itself is a critical problem, now unfolding more quickly because of the accelerated pace of the Hemlock Woolly Adelgid infestation and resurgence of the Balsam Woolly Adelgid. However, that's not the only threat to these mountains and to the narrow ribbon of asphalt that courses through it. We have met the enemy — and it is us.

Take the hike up to Humpback Rocks and enjoy the wind in your face, the sun on your cheeks and the magnificent views of the Virginia countryside below. Just don't look down at your feet too much unless you like spray paint. Ancient Native American pictographs? Not !! For some reason it has been fashionable here to leave messages on the stone about the current love of one's life; the tradition seems as strong as ever. Indian Rocks, not 40 miles down the Parkway, suffers the same affliction. It is a national disgrace.

Public outcry over the condominium development at Sugar Top Resort near Grandfather Mountain eventually led to legislation setting out height restrictions for new *building* construction — the Carolina Ridge Law. Other structures such as communication towers and windmills are unfortunately exempt. Some structures may exist for the greater good; at least that's the argument for the broadcast towers atop Mount Pisgah, visible from many miles away. Hopefully an alternative, less obtrusive solution can be devised that meets commercial needs with minimal visual impact.

Unbridled mountaintop and ridgeline development is an ongoing threat not only to Parkway view quality but to adjacent mountain areas as well. Views are in high demand. Unfortunately, cutting up a mountain top or ridgeline to have those views from a porch or picture window can ruin the view on the ridgetop above for millions of people annually. If one man's rights end where another man's face begins, what about scenic views? Living the good life is an American dream, but "hooray for me" has to be in some way balanced with these impacts and society's broader interests.

In the North Carolina mountains this is an increasingly serious problem. The fine view at Thunderstruck Ridge near

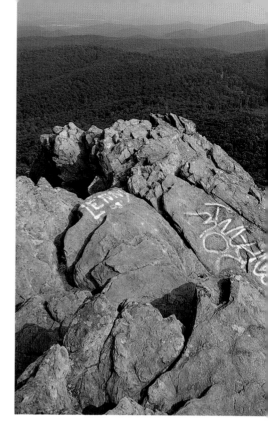
Spray paint graffiti on Humpback Rocks.

Waterrock Knob is now bespeckled with shining rooftop reflections and marred by unsightly road cuts. From the heights of Grandfather Mountain, look to the north; this is the future near Waterrock Knob unless development slows.

Why don't "they" **DO SOMETHING**? The National Park Service is unfortunately not in a strong position to intervene on many of these issues. Parkway lands constitute an easement of 125 acres per mile, averaging about 400 linear feet to each side of the road, with a few larger holdings in more developed sites.

Your National Park Service staff encourages and facilitates scenic conservation and has provided ongoing incentives to adjoining landowners with considerable success. They are available to consult

Spray paint again, this time at Indian Rocks, Indian Gap Trail, MP 47.5.

and advise on projects (which they do regularly), but rarely have direct jurisdiction.

The Park Service is under severe budgetary stress as well. Funding shortfalls left one out of three positions on the Parkway unfilled, according to a recent estimate. Recently there was only a single interpretive staffer for every 2.8 million visitors and less than 100 permanent maintenance employees for the entire 469-mile length. With critical safety issues and roadside maintenance to attend to, such niceties as grooming the overlooks often is a "when we can," not "when we would like to," proposition. Unfortunately, it's a vicious cycle. Surveys link visitor satisfaction and likelihood of returning with the quality of scenic views. Not returning means not injecting those dollars into the local economy. While that doesn't directly affect the Parkway budget, the potential fallout to the region is enormous, far exceeding maintenance and staffing costs.

YOU can make a difference. Contact your own congressional delegates as well as those from North Carolina and Virginia. Urge them to approve full funding for the Park Service and the Blue Ridge Parkway.

RISING TO THE CHALLENGE

You might think all these threats to the Parkway paint a rather bleak picture for the future, but there are many people actively working to solve these problems and make things better for the Parkway and **YOU**, its visitor. In 2004, a 28-mile section of the Parkway was designated as a "Last Chance Landscape" by Scenic America, a national nonprofit organization. **FRIENDS** of the Blue Ridge Parkway, Inc., working with the National Park Service, the Western Virginia Land Trust, Roanoke County govern-

Industrial emissions lie like morning fog in the James River Valley, as seen from the higher Parkway elevations to the south, near MP 66.

ment and others, responded by mobilizing its members and the local community to plant scores of trees to restore the visitor's visual experience in several critical areas. And that's not all they do !

- **FRIENDS** administers the Parkway's volunteer program for the National Park Service, providing over 48,276 hours of volunteer time provided by over 1,000 volunteers in 2007 alone. Based upon the federal rate of $17.55 for volunteerism, that equates to $847,244 of service given back to the Blue Ridge Parkway.
- **FRIENDS** provides trail maintenance and construction through its Trails Forever program, recruiting and coordinating volunteer efforts. Over 350 miles of Parkway trails are included. There are 100 Parkway trails and **FRIENDS** has adopted over 84 of them. As a result, the Parkway has asked **FRIENDS** to recruit volunteers to adopt intersections and overlooks in North Carolina and many are still seeking adoption. Community-based action is at the heart of **FRIENDS'** volunteer-based organization. Adopt-A-Trail and other projects like it empower community based groups along the Blue Ridge Parkway corridor to collaborate in preserving a treasure in their own backyards.
- **FRIENDS** provides support for cultural and educational programs and provides the volunteers to conduct those programs. They provide direct program materials at the Peaks of Otter Nature Center. In 2007 **FRIENDS** invested $64,161 in this effort.
- **FRIENDS** is working to help save the hemlock. The Save the Hemlock Project is one of their most challenging and rewarding projects, and they have achieved a measure of success. **FRIENDS** helps fund ongoing research into methods of adelgid control including the use of predator beetles that are similar to our familiar ladybug. The entire forest can't be saved but some areas can. Treating individual

trees with injectable insecticides works well but is labor intensive. Treated trees have over an 85% survival rate. This is a very labor intensive undertaking that requires treatment of individual trees every two to three years on an ongoing basis. **FRIENDS** helps support Park Service eradication programs. Success is measured by trees saved, not by trees lost. The need and the fight are ongoing.

- **FRIENDS** is working to help restore and rehabilitate Parkway views that have degraded for various reasons. A primary concern of visitors to the Blue Ridge Parkway is the loss of natural views. Mature trees and seedlings are planted to restore the original Parkway design elements. Each view restoration costs approximately $20,000. As the only authorized agency to restore Parkway views, **FRIENDS** has identified over 50 of them along the 469-mile Parkway that need immediate attention. The **"Save the Views"** program is an essential **FRIENDS** program. Mature trees are planted in the fall and seedlings in the spring, with plantings achieving a 98% survival rate.

- The **"Kids Empowering Kids"** program has youth and children of all ages planting some of these trees. Youth also mentor younger children to plant trees and seedlings, gain environmental awareness and share in the memories: "This is my tree—and over the years to come, I will watch it grow."

- The **"Enriching our Heritage Program"** helps protect the bog turtle, a federally listed endangered species that lives along the wetlands adjacent to the Blue Ridge Parkway. **FRIENDS** provides transmitters that track the turtles, allowing biologists to learn what parts of the wetlands the turtles use, whether they also move between other wetlands nearby, how they deal with the traffic and crossing roads, and where they spend winters.

- **FRIENDS** administers donation boxes whereby a visitor can make an immediate on the spot donation to support Parkway activities.

"Government"can't fix everything; sometimes it can't seem to fix anything. A concerted effort by concerned citizens is the single best friend the Parkway and the surrounding wild and scenic areas can possibly have. **FRIENDS** is *THE* Parkway-specific organization that is working everyday to preserve what is best about the Blue Ridge Parkway and make it better for all of us. Help preserve the Parkway for future generations. It's OK to be selfish too— help preserve it for yourself.

FRIENDS needs your voice to join over 8,000 current members. Your support is essential to continued success in meeting the many challenges that lie ahead. Consider joining **FRIENDS** of the Blue Ridge Parkway, Inc., an official Blue Ridge Parkway partner organization that provides much-needed funding and volunteers to address Parkway needs. You can visit their website and join online at www.BlueRidge-FRIENDS.org or fill out the membership form in this book and send it in. **YOU** can make a difference. Join today.

RIGHT: The many subtle shades of spring adorn a hillside near Cumberland Knob, MP 217.9.

BEST OF THE BLUE RIDGE PARKWAY

FRIENDS of the Blue Ridge Parkway, Inc, is a 501(c)(3) nonprofit corporation, orga-nized and existing under the laws of the State of North Carolina and the Common-wealth of Virginia, whose current principal business address for identification pur-poses is P.O. Box 20986, Roanoke, Virginia 24018. Tax ID #: 58-1854404. Consider leaving a Blue Ridge Parkway Legacy™ to support the Blue Ridge Parkway's Future by remembering FRIENDS in your will.

For membership information or donations, contact:
FRIENDS of the Blue Ridge Parkway, Inc.
Post Office Box 20986
Roanoke, Virginia 24018
1-800-288-PARK (7275)
www.BlueRidgeFriends.org

In 2007 **FRIENDS** provided over $1,200,000 in cash and volunteer hours to the Blue Ridge Parkway. The volunteer hours provided essential visitor services, interpre-tive and historic programs and campground hosts, positions that would otherwise have gone unfilled.

FRIENDS operates at an incredibly efficient 10% overhead. That means that 90 cents out of every dollar hits the ground running and actually **DOES SOMETHING !**

USEFUL BLUE RIDGE PARKWAY PHONE NUMBERS

MP	LOCATION
	Parkway related emergencies 1-800-PARKWATCH (1-800-727-5928)
	Parkway information 828-298-0398 (recording)
383	Parkway Headquarters 828-271-4779
6	Humpback Rocks Visitor Center 540-943-4716
60	Otter Creek Restaurant 434-299-5862
60	Otter Creek Campground 434-299-5125
86	Peaks of Otter Lodge 540-586-1081 (open year round)
86	Peaks of Otter Visitor Center 540-586-4496
115	Explore Park Visitor Center 540-427-1800
120	Roanoke Mountain Campground 540-982-9242
170	Rocky Knob Housekeeping Cabins 276-952-2947
167	Rocky Knob Visitor Center 540-745-9662
167	Rocky Knob campground 540-745-9660
176	Mabry Mill restaurant 276-952-2947
215	Blue Ridge Music Center 276-236-5309
240	Bluffs Lodge 336-372-4499
294	Cone Manor Parkway Craft Center 828-295-7938
297	Price Park Campground 828-963-5911
305	Grandfather Mountain 800-468-7325
317	Linville Falls Visitor Center 828-765-1045
317	Linville Falls Campground 828-765-7818
339	Crabtree Meadows 828-675-4236
382	Folk Art Center Parkway Information 828-298-0495
408	Pisgah Inn 828-235-8228 (seasonal)
408	Mount Pisgah Campground 828-648-2644

PARKWAY REGULATIONS AND VISITOR SAFETY

- Speed limit is 45 mph unless otherwise posted. Lower speeds are often necessary for safety reasons related to weather, visibility, pedestrian or bicycle traffic and presence of wildlife.
- Report all accidents to a Park Ranger. Call "Parkwatch" at 1-800-727-5928 (1-800-Parkwatch) to report accidents, other emergencies, fires and suspected criminal activity.
- Commercial vehicles are prohibited.
- Parking on the shoulder is permitted only if safe, and where it will not damage plants and the turf. Pull completely off the pavement.
- Fires, including charcoal, are permitted only in campgrounds and picnic areas, subject to any local fire bans in overly dry conditions.
- All plants and wildlife on the Parkway are protected. Edible fruits, nuts, and berries may be gathered for personal consumption only, except chestnuts, ginseng and pollonia which may not be taken at all.
- Pets must be on a leash or under physical control. Your pet may inadvertently harass wildlife, or be attacked by a larger predator. Clean up after your pet; have a Ziploc™ type baggie or similar device for containing pet waste near developed areas, overlooks, picnic areas and campgrounds.
- Use proper trash receptacles or take it home with you.
- Swimming is not allowed in Parkway waters.
- Fishing is allowed, subject to local regulations. A valid fishing license from Virginia or North Carolina is required, but each state's license is honored in the other state's territory in Parkway waters. A word of caution: it is easy to leave the narrow band of Parkway land without realizing it, if you are following a stream.
- Weapons are restricted in the park. It is illegal to have any loaded weapon inside the park boundaries. All weapons must be unloaded and either rendered inoperable or inaccessible. Concealed weapons are illegal on park land even if you have a state concealed weapons permit.
- Open containers of alcohol in a vehicle or in a public place are prohibited, except in designated picnic areas and campgrounds, if a registered guest.
- Gathering dead wood (that is lying on the ground only) is permitted for use as fuel in park facilities only, and only with in 300 yards of that facility.
- Camp only in campgrounds and approved backcountry sites.
- Trails are for hikers only, no bikes or motorized vehicles.

ATTENTION MOTORCYCLISTS

Parkway road design often incorporates turns of varying radius such that the turn progressively tightens as it descends. Warning signs advise of several of these descending radius spiral turns but less severe curves can be equally dangerous. Be aware of this design feature and control your speed and your bike at all times allowing an adequate safety margin for unexpected obstacles and road hazards.

DEVELOPED AREAS ALONG THE PARKWAY

⑦ Visitor Center 🚻 Comfort Station 🛏 Lodging 🏕 Picnic Area 🍴 Food Service
🥾 Hiking ⛺ Camping ♿ Wheelchair Accessible

MP	LOCATION	FACILITIES	FEATURES
5.9	Humpback Rocks	⑦ 🚻 🏕 ♿ 🥾	Humpback Mtn Farm interpretive site, Humpback Rocks
60.8	Otter Creek	⛺ 🚻 🍴 ♿ 🥾	Restaurant, campground, hiking
63	James River	⑦ 🚻 ♿ 🏕 🥾	Short hike to historic canal locks, nature trail
86	Peaks of Otter	⑦ 🛏 🍴 ⛺ 📷 🏕 ♿ 🥾	Peaks of Otter Lodge, restaurant, Nature Center, hiking, fishing, historic Johnson Farm
115	Explore Park	⑦ 🚻 🥾 ⛺ (MP 120)	The Parkway Visitor Center will remain open during Explore Park reorganization.
167	Rocky Knob	⑦ 🚻 🏕 ♿ ⛺ 🛏 🥾	Visitor center, campground, picnic area, Rocky Knob Housekeeping Cabins
176	Mabry Mill	🍴 🚻 🥾	Large historic and interpretive site with working grist mill, restaurant
215	Blue Ridge Music Center	⑦ 🚻 🏕 🎭 🥾	Outdoor amphitheater, live musical performances museum, hiking trails
240	Doughton Park	⑦ 🚻 🛏 🏕 ♿ 🍴 ⛺ 🥾	Bluffs Lodge and Coffee Shop, campground, extensive hiking trails, historic Brinegar Cabin
294	Cone Park Flat Top Manor	⑦ 🚻 ♿ 🥾	Visitor center, craft shop, hiking trails
296.7	Price Park and Lake	⛺ 📷 🏕 🚻 🥾	Fishing, canoeing, hiking, campground, picnic area
317	Linville Falls	⑦ 🚻 ⛺ 🥾 🏕	Waterfall, camping, hiking
331	Museum of NC Minerals	⑦ 🚻	Educational museum
339	Crabtree Meadows	⛺ 🍴 🏕 🚻 🥾	Restaurant, gift shop, campground, Crabtree Falls hike
355.4	Mount Mitchell State Park	🍴 ⛺ 🥾 🚻 ♿	Camping, hiking, restaurant
364	Craggy Gardens	⑦ 🚻 🏕 ♿ 🥾	Picnic area, hiking, scenery
382	Folk Art Center	⑦ 🚻 ♿	Craft & Art Galleries, gift shop
408	Mount Pisgah	🛏 🍴 ⛺ 🚻 ♿	Pisgah Inn, campground
451	Waterrock Knob	⑦ 🚻 🥾	Visitor center, hiking, views

PARKWAY TUNNEL CLEARANCES

Drivers of RV's and those towing large trailers should be aware of tunnel clearances along your selected route, and the escape route if one is needed due to severe weather conditions. NC 226 north to Spruce Pine, MP 330.9 is gentle, but steep in the other direction towards Marion. U.S. 221 south to Marion at Linville Falls is steep at first, but levels out after about 4 miles. NC 226A at Little Switzerland is easier than NC 226 at Gillespie Gap south to Marion, but neither is easy. South of Asheville, the main crossing roads, U.S. 276 and NC 215 are steep winding challenging mountain roads, though they are paved. This is white knuckle driving with a big rig. U.S. 23-74 at Balsam Gap MP 443 is mellow; U.S. 19 at Soco Gap MP 455.7 descends steeply at first, but then flattens out. NOTE THE LOWER CLEARANCES BETWEEN SOCO GAP AND THE SMOKIES !!

MP	NAME	CENTER STRIPE CLEARANCE	CLEARANCE AT SHOULDER
53.1	Bluff Mountain	19'1"	13'7"
333.4	Little Switzerland	19' 8"	14' 4"
336.8	Wildacres	19' 10"	13' 1"
344.5	Twin Tunnel #1	21' 0"	16' 0"
344.7	Twin Tunnel #2	19' 7"	14' 7"
349.0	Rough Ridge	21' 6"	13' 9"
364.4	Craggy Pinnacle	19' 9"	14' 1"
365.5	Craggy Flats	19' 5"	14' 4"
374.4	Tanbark Ridge	19' 5"	14' 1"
397.1	Grassy Knob	19' 2"	13' 7"
399.1	Pine Mountain	19' 3"	14' 2"
400.9	Ferrin Knob #1	19' 6"	14' 2"
401.3	Ferrin Knob #2	19' 2"	14' 0"
401.5	Ferrin Knob #3	19' 5"	13' 9"
403.0	Young Pisgah Ridge	19' 8"	14' 6"
404.0	Fork Mountain	19' 2"	14' 0"
406.9	Little Pisgah	19' 5"	13' 10"
407.3	Buck Spring	19' 2"	13' 3"
410.1	Frying Pan	19' 9"	13' 8"
422.1	Devil's Courthouse	19' 0"	14' 2"
439.7	Pinnacle Ridge	19' 1"	13' 10"
458.8	Lickstone Ridge	18' 1"	**11' 1"**
459.3	Bunches Bald	18' 4"	**10' 6"**
461.2	Big Witch	18' 1"	**11' 3"**
465.6	Rattlesnake Mountain	19' 6"	14' 5"
466.2	Sherrill Cove	19' 7"	14' 4"

ADDITIONAL READING and RESOURCES

If you stacked all the books and other publications written about the Blue Ridge Parkway on top of each other, it would give you a stack likely taller than the average 4 year old, and would weigh more as well. You could spend the weekend at the Ritz for what they would cost you. That was in fact, one of the reasons for this book—an attempt to consolidate the abundance of information as well as offer a new look and approach to the Parkway. I have used the following books and found them to be very informative and helpful in my travels and think you will as well. This is by no means an all inclusive list.

Several useful and free publications are available at the visitor centers and in nearby towns. The Park Service foldout map and guide was the template for the chapter maps in this book, and is packed with additional information. Each visitor center has area trail maps and other informative brochures. The free *Blue Ridge Parkway Directory and Travel Planner*, published by the Blue Ridge Parkway Association, details many privately owned facilities in nearby towns including restaurants, hotels and campgrounds. The free *Blue Ridge Parkway / Smokies Travel Guide*, published by Leisure Publishing, is packed with loads of useful area travel information. Call toll free, 800-548-1672, or order online at www.blueridgeparkwayusa.com.

ADDITIONAL READING

Blue Ridge Parkway Guide: Rockfish Gap to Grandfather Mountain and Blue Ridge Parkway Guide: Grandfather Mountain to Great Smoky Mountains National Park by William G. Lord. Taken together, this series gives more in depth history than you will find anywhere. Mr. Lord tells you how each place was named, and provides tons of lore and history that would have otherwise been lost, all milepost by milepost. It's the classic work about the story of these lands and the people that called the Parkway home.

Super-Scenic Motorway: A Blue Ridge Parkway History by Anne Mitchell Whisnant. This book gives and in depth look at the social forces, politics and controversies surrounding the conception and construction of the Parkway. This makes fascinating reading for anyone who wants to delve more deeply into that aspect of Parkway history.

The Blue Ridge Parkway by Harley E. Jolley – The original Parkway history book. First published in 1969, it preserves insights that would have otherwise faded from memory.

Blue Ridge Parkway Wonder and Light by Jerry D. Greer and Ian Plant – Wonderful images by two of the Blue Ridge's most talented photographers.

OFF-PARKWAY FOREST SERVICE AND WILDERNESS INFORMATION.

George Washington National Forest
www.fs.fed.us/r8/gwj/gp/
Glenwood / Pedlar Ranger Districts
540-291-2188

Pisgah National Forest
www.cs.unca.edu/nfsnc/
Grandfather Ranger District
828-652-2144
Pisgah Ranger District 828-877-3265
Cradle of Forestry 828-877-3130
www.cradleofforestry.com/

EPILOGUE

The twilight sky — the setting sun is chased by a crescent moon – tail lights streak by on their way to who-knows-where. Moments like these are beyond price, the chance meeting of all these elements at just the right nexus in time. This scene unfolded in my rearview mirror as I drove to Roanoke from Mabry Mill. Frantically seeking a safe place to turn around, I hastily reversed course to photograph in the fading light. When you think its over, or there's nothing there, BAM! — it hits you. The Parkway is like that — something beautiful, something cool — every foot, every mile. Just be there.

As the final pages are written and laid up, and the production pace slows, I can reflect on all the wondrous events I have been privileged to witness during the years that went into making this book. I hope Best of the Blue Ridge Parkway conveys what is unique and wonderful about this special place and helps guide you through your travels. May all your days be filled with light.

Nye is a writer-photographer living in Knoxville, Tennessee, in the shadow of the Great Smoky Mountains, near the southern end of the Blue Ridge Parkway. Photographing and writing about the Southern Appalachian Mountains provides him an avenue of expression and an opportunity to share his experiences with you. Published in regional and national publications, his ongoing emphasis is classic landscape photography. He still works with color films using the traditional 4x5-inch view camera, supplemented by digital photographic imaging. This is his 4th book. Previous titles include *Tennessee Wonder and Light, the Smoky Mountains Photographer's Guide* (with Bill Campbell) and *Great Smoky Mountains Wonder and Light* (with Jerry Greer and Bill Lea).

You can find him online at www.SimmonsPhotoArts.com